To my grandchildren Ethan Van Horn,
Mallory Lindsey, and Ashley Lindsey,
from Pop Pop

Contents

List of Tables, Charts, and Map

LIST OF TABLES

CHARTS

MAP

Acknowledgments

I am grateful to David Wilson for creating the book's charts, tables, and maps. David is the coordinator of educational media, Center for Instruction and Research Technology, University of North Florida–Jacksonville.

Special thanks are also due to Bruce Smith, editor of *Phi Delta Kappan, Journal for Education,* for his kind words and for writing the forward. Bruce knows what's good for kids; therefore, his support over many years has been especially meaningful.

It would have been impossible to do the research for this book without the powerful online tools, databases, and citation software provided by the Carpenter Library at the university. Although we are a modest-size university, we have online research tools that rival those of any Research One institution.

I would also like to thank all my friends and colleagues who read rough drafts of the chapters. Neighbor and friend Pam Eason gave many thoughtful suggestions. She read the book as an interested layperson. Colleagues who were especially helpful and supportive include Sandra Gupton, Alan Seagren, Don Kauchak, William W. Purkey, and Phil Riner.

Foreword

Everything in this book is subject to revision. But I didn't need to tell you that. If you're like most readers, you've already glanced ahead at the opening pages before you took the time to read what some commentator has to say in the Foreword. And it's right there in Royal Van Horn's first sentence: "This book is about science." Just about the only thing in science that remains constant is that it's always changing, in ways large and small, as we acquire new information and as old understandings and explanations are disconfirmed.

Of course, that's one of the singular strengths of science, but it's also a major source of its complexity. And while complexity is a necessary evil in trying to explain the workings of the natural and human-made worlds, it is a definite handicap when science meets public policy. Schools, public and private, constitute one area of public policy that directly touches some 35 percent of U.S. households. When education science seeks to move out of the realm of the research journals and into the arena of public policy, even those of us with a direct interest in education—parents, teachers, school administrators, and surprisingly a great many professors of education—could use a little help in sorting things out. In short, we could use a translator.

And Royal Van Horn is, above all else, a translator—and a highly experienced one. Since September 1994, he has written the Technology column (in those days known as Power Tools) for the *Phi Delta Kappan*, a magazine I've been editing throughout those years, and translation and explanation are among the primary goals of that column. For if anything changes as fast as science, it's that first-generation spin-off of scientific investigation, technology. Each month, Royal examines the ever-changing landscape of technology—from videodiscs way back when in the 1980s to iPhones just yesterday to heaven only knows what else tomorrow. He takes readers by the hand and shows them what's new, what it's good for, and whether it's worth it.

The experience of making the complex comprehensible eminently qualifies him to take on a task like writing *Words on Fire*. For this book is first and foremost an exercise in surveying a complex landscape, finding the nuggets of gold, and refining them into a form that can be used by general readers with an interest in education. The topics treated in *Words on Fire*—from retention in grade to early childhood education to high-stakes testing—all have direct implications for public policy, the public purse, and the future of our democracy. It's crucial that citizens and their elected leaders make decisions in these areas with the backing of the strongest scientific evidence available.

But if that kind of sound deliberation is to take place, both the public and policymakers need to know which measures are supported by solid educational research and which are not. In *Words on Fire*, Royal Van Horn surveys the original research, compiles its findings, and presents those findings in an easily comprehended form. But more than that, whenever possible, he lets the researchers speak for themselves. In brief and well-chosen snippets—dubbed appropriately enough, "Words on Fire"—the members of the research community show that sometimes they, too, can speak clearly and directly.

Perhaps the term "educational malpractice" will strike some readers as too highly charged for a research report, but when the enormous accumulation of research on grade retention shows consistently negative effects on both the achievement and emotional health of children, researcher Shane Jimerson minces no words. Neither does Royal Van Horn. And when you've read this book and the topic arises at a neighborhood barbecue or at a game day tailgating party or at a local school board meeting, neither should you.

Bruce Smith, Editor
Phi Delta Kappan

1

Knowing About Education

This book is about science. This book is not about belief. What you know—or think you know—about education may not be true. People's beliefs are often so strong that even in the face of overwhelming evidence to the contrary, they cling to their beliefs. If you hold your beliefs dear and don't want to change them, this book may be disquieting. On the other hand, if you can keep an open mind, then this book is for you.

When people think of science, they think of the natural sciences, such as physics or medicine. This book is about the social sciences, and in particular about education science. Although it is difficult to know whether more research is done in the natural sciences or in the social sciences, one thing is certain: there is a massive body of scientific research in the social sciences, and a lot of children would be better off if the results of this research were more widely known.

WORDS ON FIRE

People often speak about the human condition, but some speak with *Words on Fire*. Education scientists are often eloquent and pointed when they describe their findings. The *Words on Fire* sections of this book are direct quotes taken from the research literature. The *Words on Fire* are NOT the author's words.

FIVE CULTURES

As it relates to education science, there are five fairly distinct groups of people.

Education Scientist

The people who do educational research are a large, but often unknown group. They tend to talk mostly to one another, attend conferences with fellow researchers, and publish their research findings in limited-circulation journals that are often unread by anyone other than fellow researchers. By and large, education scientists do not feel compelled to interpret their research to the layperson. They often take the stance that it is enough work to do the research.

Research Consumers

Some educators are avid consumers of educational research. People in this relatively small group make it a habit to find, read, compare, and interpret educational research. Reading and evaluating educational research is more difficult than it might seem since many research studies are dozens of pages long and often full of statistics. It would seem logical that professors of education would be in this group, but they usually are not. Admittedly, some professors of education are research consumers, but they are a small minority.

Education Professors

Education professors spend substantial amounts of their time training future and practicing teachers, principals, and superintendents. Often they are so involved in helping teachers-to-be prepare for the day when they will have their own classroom or school that they often have little time to be consumers of education science. There is no hard data, but the percentage of education professors who are avid consumers of education science is probably less than 30 percent. This is unfortunate because their students and the lay public think that education professors know the research.

Practitioners

Teachers, principals, and superintendents are involved in teaching children and managing schools. These are challenging jobs, and they are often stressful. Their main source of information about education science is the local newspaper, television news, and nonresearch-oriented journals. When they were students, these people probably erroneously thought that their college professors were consumers of education science.

The Lay Public

Parents, taxpayers, elected school-board members, politicians, and policymakers generally decide how schools should operate and how children should be taught. By and large, these people are not consumers of educational research, so their decisions are often based on their beliefs, their intuition, and even their political leanings.

Obviously, many people are members of several of the groups already mentioned. *Words on Fire* is written for people who have had neither the time nor inclination to study education science.

WAYS OF KNOWING

We develop our understanding of—and thereby make our decisions about—schools and teaching in several ways. Examining how we know something is important since different ways of knowing have different characteristics.

Personal Experience

In education and in child rearing, we often depend on our personal experience to know what is best. For example, most teachers know from experience when they are losing a class and when it is time to change an activity. Obviously, personal experience is limited to what we have seen and observed. I often ask my graduate students what grade they would give the local schools. The most frequent grades they give are Bs and Cs with a few Ds. The point is, there are 140 local schools, and the students have given them grades based on visiting or teaching in only a few of them. The students may not have much personal experience, but they are always quick to weigh in on the topic.

Tradition

Often we do things because we have always done them that way. For example, schools run on an agrarian calendar with several months off in the summer. One hundred years ago, this was important because the children had to help harvest the crops. Today, less than 5 percent of the population farms. Because of this agrarian school calendar, changing to a year-round school schedule is resisted. The summer break or vacation actually hurts poor children since they typically lose ground, or backslide, over the summer. This is not true for middle income and affluent children who usually do enriching things, such as take vacations over the summer. "Because we have always done it that way," may not be the best for the children.

Experts

In education, as is true in any profession, there are experts. Experts usually have more experience in a particular area than most educators, so they are sought out for their knowledge and skills. Often, however, two experts might disagree on how a complex educational problem should be solved. Presumably, experts are intimately familiar with the research literature, but this is not always the case. For example, a local school board hired a keynote speaker who was supposedly an expert on the Third International Math and Science (TIMMs) comparisons to kick off the school year. According to the expert, the United States was falling behind the rest of the world in the areas of science and math. Unfortunately, the expert based his speech on a rank ordering of the nations. The actual differences in the scores of the United States and other countries were, in fact, insignificant. This is analogous to saying that the third-place performer in an Olympic event is a poor athlete.

Research Evidence

Unlike the above ways of knowing, which are subjective, research is objective. Since the education of the approximately 46 million children in the United States is important, studying the accumulated body of knowledge—the research—is also important. Many things that people think they know about schools and children are simply not true. When studied systematically, education science can be used to develop understandings that are not based on opinion, hearsay, limited experience, or tradition.

THE NATURE OF SCIENCE

Science is both a body of knowledge and a process for acquiring new knowledge. Because science is ongoing, our knowledge of the world improves over time. One of the most important scientific processes is replication. Scientists do research and publish it so that other scientists can conduct similar research that will either verify or refute the first scientist's work. After this process continues through many repetitions, what is suspected becomes more certain. For example, many issues that have arisen from over 100 scientific studies have become topics in this book.

A second attribute of science is that most research reports are published in juried or refereed journals. That means that before a research article is published, it is sent to an anonymous group of social scientists who have expertise similar to the author's. This blind-review process ensures that biased and/or unsound research generally does not get published. Many research journals are so selective that their acceptance rate is less than 10 percent.

A third attribute of science is that it is ongoing. Science evolves over time. It is not static. Over time, our understanding of children and schools grows. If you think about this, you might come to the conclusion that the information in this book will soon be out of date. That would be true except that most of the topics discussed in the book have already been studied for many years.

A fourth attribute of science makes it important to keep in mind that most educational research studies groups of children—often very large groups. Thus the research can tell us what is best for *most* children, but it cannot tell us how to deal with each and every child. This is because each child is a unique human being. The research does, however, tell us how to deal with the vast majority of children. Unless there is a very good reason to not deal with children in the way the research suggests, we should follow the research. An example will be explained in chapter 2: Flunking Kids/Grade Retention. If a teacher decides to retain a child at grade level, that teacher is acting contrary to the evidence that it is harmful to children. In a sense, the retaining teacher is going out on a limb.

GENERALIZING

All the students at a particular grade level are called the "population" of children. At each grade level, there are approximately four million children. Obviously, researchers cannot study this huge group of children; therefore, they study a sample of the population. The question then becomes, Are the children in this sample of children truly representative of the whole population? An example would be, if a particular research study was conducted in a large urban area, are the students there like students from small towns or rural areas? Research that has been replicated using widely varying samples of children greatly helps us generalize the research.

In some ways, children everywhere are alike, but they are also different. For example, children everywhere have similar fears. In contrast, children in the inner city have different recreational activities than children in rural areas do. Most educational research, however, examines attributes of children that are generally believed to be similar across widely varying populations.

AFFILIATION BIAS

If an organization, business, or political-interest group reports on research it sponsored or created, it is important to worry about whether the research is biased. Obviously, people who are employed or sponsored by an organization feel an obligation to promote the organization's agenda or to work toward its best interests. Indeed, some organizations purposely create research, or quasi-research, designed to support their political agenda. Estimates vary, but there are approximately 200 political-interest groups in the United States, and some of them create this quasi-research. Two of the most well known are the American Heritage Foundation and the Hudson Institute. Unfortunately, the popular press often reports the results of this research without carefully considering *who* did the research. Even generally reputable sources such as the *New York Times* and National Public Radio occasionally report on such research without commenting on the credibility of the source. Reputable educational journals try to guard against this kind of bias, therefore, they are better sources of unbiased information.

Although it is not common, some doctoral dissertations have affiliation bias. Doctoral students work closely with the chairperson of their dissertation committee, and they may feel obliged to do research that makes their major professor happy. One well-known educational-reform movement has had more than 125 research studies conducted on its effectiveness. The reform author's own doctoral students, however, did 85 of these studies. Careful readers of educational research always check the affiliation of the author(s). One can generally find the affiliation of the author(s) in the fine print somewhere on the first page of the research report.

THE U.S. DEPARTMENT OF EDUCATION

The president appoints the U.S. Secretary of Education. The same is true for the deputy and undersecretaries. Obviously the president is likely to appoint a secretary who has political beliefs similar to his. For example, soon after George W. Bush became president, the Department of Education's (DOE) Education Resources Information Center (ERIC) published several *ERIC Briefs* that were slanted—or biased—summaries of the research on charter schools—a favorite idea of many conservative Republicans. (A liberal president would likely have made similar appointments.)

Mitigating this potential political bias in the DOE is that the U.S. DOE is a giant organization with many branches, some of which are only slightly subject to political influence. The most reliable and trustworthy branch of the department is the National Center for Education Statistics (NCES). The only thing one has to be careful to do when examining NCES data and research is to read how they define their variables. For example, the NCES reports the age of a school building based on the last time it was remodeled or had an addition. So a 60-year-old school with a new cafeteria would show up as being only as old as the cafeteria. Another example of an idiosyncratic variable is the definition of a "high school dropout." To the NCES, any person who passes the Graduate Equivalency Degree (GED) test by age 22 is not a high school dropout.

Great care was taken in this book to avoid the use of biased research or misleading statistics.

MISTAKES IN REASONING

In education, as in other areas, mistakes in reasoning are common. People concerned about schools and children need to guard against making these mistakes. One of the common mistakes is the "compared to what?" mistake. For example, in a recent international comparison of education in developed countries, it was noted that nine of the top-ten nations had a national curriculum. A national curriculum is one in which every child in every school in the country learns the same thing at the same grade level. On the surface, this sounds like a convincing argument for implementing a national curriculum in the United States. Nine of the bottom-ten countries in the world, however, also had a national curriculum.

Another common mistake is to believe the math theorem, if $A = B$ and $B = C$, then $A = C$. This works in math, but not in education science. In education, the link between A and B and the link between B and C are often both weak. Two weak links do not make a strong chain. In mathematical terms, if the relationship between A and B is .20 and the relationship between B and C is also .20, then the relationship between A and C is $.20 \times .20$, or .04

Still another common mistake is confusing statistical significance with practical significance. For example, in a very well done study, it was found that students who had sex-education courses had their first sexual experience significantly earlier than students who had not had a sex-education course. The practical significance, however, was 61 days. Do you suppose it makes much difference to a parent if their child loses their virginity on June 1 or August 1 of the same summer? I think not.

An idea closely related to practical significance is strength of effect. Strength of effect is simply a matter of finding out how much a change in one thing affects another thing. For example, adopting a new reading curriculum might improve the reading scores of children. The important question is not, does it make a difference? Rather, the important question is, does it make enough difference to justify buying all the new materials and training all the teachers to use the new program? Research often finds things that make a difference, but the wise person asks, how much difference does it make?

Evaluation Research

In publications such as this one, it is customary to specify what is not included. Evaluation research examines the effectiveness of textbooks, reading programs, education-reform efforts, organizations like the Parent Teacher's Association (PTA), and projects like DARE (Drug Abuse Resistance Education). With the exception of a few studies described in chapter 4, evaluation research is not a major theme of this book. Nonetheless, the reader should know that it exists and that it needs to be given more attention.

Here is why. Marketing and selling things to schools is big—really big—business. For example, a single textbook might cost $50. If a school district has a few thousand students, then a few thousand textbooks cost a lot of money. Furthermore, some state departments of education make statewide textbook adoptions. Imagine the statewide cost of such decisions. Textbook publishers have massive marketing teams who work diligently to persuade schools that their textbooks are the best available. Rarely do educators ask to see evaluation research that demonstrates the effectiveness of a textbook or of a reading or math series. By and large, educators make purchasing decisions based on their personal impressions of the book.

EDUCATIONAL POLICY

This book is about educational research, which should inform educational policy. Studying the research helps us understand why some educational policy works and some does not. In order to not bias the discussion of the research, however, a discussion of the policy implications of the research is reserved for the last chapter.

INERTIA

Education is the largest enterprise in the country. As such, it is a massive endeavor that keeps moving forward. Due to the magnitude of the enterprise, it has a massive amount of inertia. Even small course corrections are difficult to make happen. Hopefully the education science herein will help better direct the enterprise.

2

Flunking Kids/Grade Retention

These days, we hear so much about the importance of education and of "leaving no child behind." It is time to take a close look at traditional educational practices and to reevaluate their effectiveness. The flunking of kids in school, or grade retention, as it is more-professionally labeled, is almost universally believed to be beneficial to children. Scientific evidence, however, refutes this belief.

After a thorough review of the research evidence, a pair of researchers stated the following:

WORDS ON FIRE

Those who continue to retain pupils at grade level do so despite cumulative research evidence showing that the potential for negative effects consistently outweighs positive outcomes. Because this cumulative evidence consistently points to the negative effects of non-promotion, the burden of proof legitimately falls on proponents of retention plans to show there is compelling logic indicating success of their plans when so many other plans have failed. (Holmes and Matthews 1984, 235)

In order to understand the huge body of research on grade retention, it is necessary to have a rudimentary understanding of the two techniques used to summarize the findings of the many research studies done on the topic. The first and simplest method is vote counting. In this method, only the studies that agree or disagree with the given premise are counted (i.e., 20 studies said one thing and six said another). The second and more preferable method of combining studies is known as meta-analysis. Essentially, meta-analysis is a relatively simple technique that averages the positive and negative findings of various studies. As a simple example, if one study shows a very large positive effect and another shows a small negative effect, the first study would be given more weight.

The easiest way to understand effect size, which is the amount a situation is changed when a research variable is added or subtracted, is to see how various effect sizes relate to percentiles. Percentile is a common scale used in education. It goes from 1 to 99. Percentile means, ". . . did better than that percent of the population." For example, a student at 40 percentile did better on the measurement than 40 percent of the other students. Table 2.1 shows how large various effect sizes are in terms of percentile. You will notice in table 2.1 that even a small effect size of .3 makes a big difference in a student's percentile scores.

A second way to visualize effect size is shown below. On the percentile scale, the distance between the 16 percentile and the 50 percentile is one standard deviation. Likewise, the distance between the 50 percentile and the 84 percentile is also one standard deviation. The area between the 16 percentile and the 84 percentile is called "average." As you move from the 50 percentile downward, you get closer and closer to "below average," which is the 16 percentile. As you move from the 50 percentile upward, you get closer and closer

Table 2.1 Examples of Percentile Gains for Various Effect Sizes		
Effect size	From percentile	To percentile
1.0	16	50
0.5	16	33
0.4	16	30
0.3	16	26

to "above average," which is the 84 percentile. The asterisk on the scale below shows an effect size of .5 standard deviations. A positive effect size of .5 would move a child from 16 percentile to the asterisk, which is 33 percentile.

16 percentile———*——50 percentile————————84 percentile

In the last 25 years, there have been three major meta-analysis studies examining the effects of retention: Holmes and Matthews (1984); Holmes (1989); and Jimerson (2001). In an effort to understand the facts about grade retention, a short summary of the findings of each of these studies is presented. The summaries are then followed by a discussion of what the combined studies reveal.

HOLMES AND MATTHEWS
META-ANALYSIS, 1984 (44 STUDIES)

After an exhaustive review of the research literature, and after using tight selection criteria, Holmes and Matthews found 44 studies. Thirty-one of these studies compared the academic achievement of retained students with the achievement of a group of similar children who had been promoted. The researchers found a combined effect size of −.44 for the retained children. In other words, "The promoted group of children on average had achieved .44 standard deviations higher than the retained group" (p. 229).

When the researchers combined the results of 21 studies that had examined the effects of retention on measures of personal adjustment, they found an effect size of −.27. In other words, "Retained students scored an average of .27 standard deviations lower than promoted students" (p. 230). See table 2.1.

In educational research, effect sizes of this magnitude, when summed across so many studies, are most uncommon and highly persuasive. The next two studies show even more evidence of the negative effects of retention.

HOLMES META-ANALYSIS, 1989 (63 STUDIES)

In 1989, Holmes surveyed the research on grade retention that had been done since his and Matthews's 1984 analysis. He found an additional 19 studies, which he included with the original 44 studies, for a total of 63 studies covering the years from 1925 to 1989. The 63 studies compared retained students with similar students who were promoted. Of the 63 studies, Holmes reported that 54 studies reported negative achievement effects when retained children went on to the next grade. Of the nine studies that reported positive short-term effects, the benefits diminished over time and disappeared in later grades. The overall effect size of retention on achievement in this 1989 analysis was −.19, as compared to the earlier effect size of −.44.

WORDS ON FIRE

The weight of empirical evidence argues against retention. (Holmes 1989, 28)

JIMERSON META-ANALYSIS, 1999 (20 STUDIES)

At first glance, it appears that the trend is toward less difference between retained students and similar promoted students. The third meta-analysis done by Shane Jimerson (2001), however, adds even more evidence to the negative effects of retention.

After a systematic literature search, Jimerson found 20 research studies published between 1990 and 1999. In total, these studies looked at more than 1,100 retained students and more than 1,500 promoted students. One of Jimerson's criteria for including a study in his analysis was the use of an identifiable and appropriate comparison group of promoted students who were matched on variables such as intelligence, achievement, socioemotional adjustment, socioeconomic status, and gender. Jimerson's effect size for overall academic achievement was −.39, which again favored the promoted students. The effect size for language arts was −.36, reading was −.54, and mathematics was −.49. The effect size for socioemotional adjustment was −.22.

WORDS ON FIRE

Thus, the results yielded from recent reviews and meta-analysis provide converging prima fascia evidence suggesting a strong case could be made for grade retention as "educational malpractice" given that research has failed to

demonstrate the effectiveness of grade retention as an academic intervention.
(Jimerson 2004, in Walberg 2004, 82)

Obviously, there is a current, massive body of scientific evidence showing that retained children, when compared to similar children who are promoted, are harmed by the practice of retaining.

INTERVIEWS WITH RETAINED CHILDREN

Most parents and teachers believe that retention is not traumatic or stigmatizing to children. Children, however, have a much different view. Deborah Byrnes (Shepard 1989; Smith 1989) interviewed 71 retained children in grades 1, 3, and 5. There were 52 first graders, 9 third graders, and 10 sixth graders. More first graders were interviewed because retention is more common in the lower grades. In addition, more boys were interviewed than girls were because boys are retained more often. To ensure that the retained students did not know the purpose of the interviews, the researcher interviewed the children in groups of three; in each group, there was only one child who had been retained.

Interestingly, of the 71 interviewed children, only 57 percent of the girls named themselves as being retained compared to 81 percent of the boys. When asked how they felt about being retained, 84 percent of the answers mentioned feeling "sad, bad, or upset" (p. 116). Only 6 percent of the children reported positive feelings. The researcher also interviewed non-retained children. When asked what they thought would be the worst thing about being retained, they responded, "being laughed at or teased" (22 percent), "not being with friends" (14 percent), "being sad" (10 percent), "getting bad grades" (8 percent) (p. 129). Several retained children mentioned that they did not want their birthdays to come since they would have to tell their age.

Even more devastating was that the children not only had to cope at school with the pressures and social stigma of retention, but they also were frequently punished and penalized at home for being retained.

IN THE WORDS OF RETAINED CHILDREN

Researcher: "Were you punished at all?"

Angela (first grade): They were mad and real sad. They spanked me and [I was] grounded. I didn't get to go to Disneyland.

Tommy (first grade): Mad! Dad paddled me and kicked me out of the house.

Miguel (first grade): They were sad. They said, "Be good at school."

Will (first grade): They didn't care. They were mad at school because the teacher didn't teach me barely anything.

Veronica (third grade): Mad! They said I didn't try hard. No TV for a month. I couldn't go anywhere. I got grounded.

Carol (third grade): They were okay. They hope I pass this year.

Robert (sixth grade): They were mad. They said that I better pass 'cause I need a good education.

Note: Out of the 71 students interviewed, 47 percent said they were punished for being retained.

From: Byrnes, D. 1989. Attitude of students, parents, and educators toward repeating a grade. In L.S. Shepard and M.L. Smith (Eds). Flunking grades: research and policies on retention. New York: Falmer Press: 117–18.

TEACHER BELIEFS: DEVELOPMENTAL STAGE

According to Mary Lee Smith (Shepard 1989; Smith 1989), almost all teachers believe that retention is good, but for different reasons. Smith conducted structured interviews with forty kindergarten teachers and found that teachers' beliefs about retention fell into one of four categories. Nineteen of the 40 teachers were classified as "nativists." Nativists believed that, ". . . children become prepared for school according to an evolutionary, physiological unfolding of abilities. This process, which unfolds in stages, is largely outside the influence of parents and teachers. The only thing teachers can do to help the child who is currently in a developmental stage that is not appropriate for kindergarten is to allow more time for the child to develop, and if possible, to remove the child from the stresses of a developmentally appropriate environment" (p. 136). As one teacher put it, "Sometimes you just have to wait and let Mother Nature catch up and help the child."

The remaining 21 teachers, who did not express a belief in Developmental Stage, had a mixture of beliefs about retention. One group of teachers believed in the remediation, which they *thought* was bound to happen when a grade level was repeated.

WORDS ON FIRE

[Teachers do not receive] feedback on what happens to retained children later in their school careers. A taller and quieter retained child may not seem too out of place in the early grades. But what about the fifth-grade boy who can shave, the junior high school student who can drive himself to school, the pubescent third grader, those who can vote or be drafted before finishing high school, the adult who no longer feels at home in a high school built for adolescents? (Smith in Shepard 1989; Smith 1989, 148)

RETENTION AND SCHOOL DROPOUTS

Karl Alexander and other researchers spent over twenty years conducting The Beginning School Study (BSS) (Alexander, Entwisle, Dauber, and Kabbani, in Walberg 2004). The BSS followed children who started first grade in 20 Baltimore public schools in 1982. In 2004, they published the research report "Dropout in Relation to Grade Retention." After rigorous statistical analyses of a massive amount of data, they reported that retained children are many times more likely to drop out than non-retained children (p. 17). See chart 2.1, Dropout Risks by Retention Status. Notice that children who were never retained had a 24 percent chance of dropping out of school while retained students had a 67.3 percent chance of dropping out. Students retained twice, who were not in special-education classes, had an 89 percent chance of dropping out.

The public is often confused by the way school districts report data like the data mentioned earlier. Instead of publishing graduation rates, many districts report dropout rates. For example, a school district might report a high school dropout rate of 5 percent. This makes it look as though 95 percent of their students graduate. A dropout rate, however, is a recurring percent of nongraduating students per year. A dropout rate of 5 percent means that 5 percent this year will not graduate, 5 percent next year, and so on.

In October 2004, Jing Miao and Walt Haney of Boston College published an extensive study entitled "High School Graduation Rates." Table 2.2 from their study shows state-by-state graduation rates for

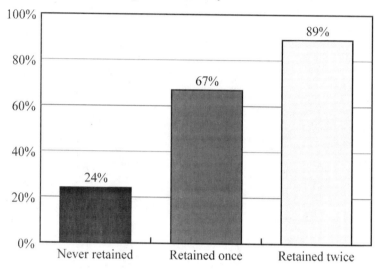

Chart 2.1 Drop Out Risk by Retention Status

Adapted from Alexander, et. al., 2004 p18

Blacks, Hispanics, and Whites. Pay close attention to the three columns in table 2.2. Each of the table's three columns shows states with the lowest graduation rates for each group on the top of a column.

These figures are listed as "means" because each number is an average of the five different ways these kinds of data are computed. According to the researchers, there are three reasons why no rates were reported for some states. Some states do not report graduation rates by race. In addition, certain states have too few students of a particular race to be considered. Montana, for example, reported graduating only 33 African American students in 2001. Finally, if a state reported a graduation rate of over 110 percent, their data or calculations were suspect.

WORDS ON FIRE

One principle or standard seems fundamental: an intervention intended to help should do no harm, and there can be no doubt that [the] elevated dropout

Table 2.2 Individual State Graduation Rates by Race (Class 2001)

Black	Mean	Hispanic	Mean	White	Mean
NY	45.4%	NY	41.6%	FL	61.3%
WI	45.9%	GA	48.0%	GA	62.7%
GA	47.4%	DE	50.1%	HI	63.9%
FL	48.9%	NV	51.0%	MS	64.4%
HI	49.9%	MA	52.7%	KY	67.0%
IN	50.9%	CO	52.8%	AL	68.0%
IL	50.9%	OR	53.6%	AK	68.1%
OH	51.9%	CT	53.7%	WA	68.6%
KY	52.3%	PA	54.9%	OR	70.1%
MN	53.5%	WA	55.4%	LA	71.7%
NV	53.8%	FL	56.6%	NV	72.2%
OR	55.3%	MI	58.5%	NC	72.5%
MI	55.4%	KS	59.6%	DE	74.3%
WA	55.8%	AL	59.6%	RI	74.6%
AL	57.3%	MN	60.0%	WY	75.3%
CO	57.6%	IL	60.1%	NM	75.4%
NE	57.9%	CA	60.5%	IN	75.5%
DE	57.9%	HI	60.9%	ME	75.9%
MS	57.9%	TX	61.2%	CO	75.9%
NC	59.5%	WY	61.8%	OK	76.1%
LA	59.5%	NM	62.2%	WV	76.5%
MO	59.6%	WI	62.2%	AR	76.6%
PA	59.7%	OH	63.0%	TX	76.7%
CT	60.1%	AK	64.4%	NY	77.2%
IA	60.6%	RI	65.5%	MO	77.4%
CA	60.6%	IA	65.5%	VA	77.4%
AK	62.4%	IN	65.9%	CA	77.5%
KS	62.5%	NE	66.5%	MI	78.0%
TX	64.1%	NC	67.1%	MA	79.4%
OK	65.2%	UT	67.4%	MD	79.5%
WV	66.5%	OK	71.3%	CT	81.4%
MA	67.6%	AR	74.2%	KS	82.0%
AR	67.9%	VA	76.0%	OH	82.3%
UT	68.1%	MD	76.4%	MT	83.5%
VA	68.2%	LA	76.6%	IL	83.6%
MD	70.1%	MO	79.5%	UT	84.5%
NM	71.5%	KY	81.4%	PA	84.5%
RI	73.4%	MT	94.0%	MN	85.5%
AZ	n/a	AZ	n/a	IA	85.7%
ID	n/a	ID	n/a	SD	86.3%
NH	n/a	ME	n/a	WI	86.8%
NJ	n/a	MS	n/a	NE	87.6%
SC	n/a	ND	n/a	ND	89.1%
TN	n/a	NH	n/a	NJ	99.5%

Adapted from Miano & Haney, 2004

risk of the magnitude seen in these results qualifies as "Harm." (Alexander et al. 2004, 20)

A LIFETIME OF LOWER WAGES

As we have previously seen, many retained students drop out of school. When a student drops out of high school, they generally have consigned themselves to a lifetime of lower wages than those of students who graduate. Chart 2.2, taken from the latest U.S. census data, shows the median annual income for males (black or blue bars) and females (gray bars) who did and did not complete high school. Notice that a male high school graduate will earn $13,362 more per year than one who does not complete ninth grade. Thus a male who does not complete ninth grade will make $400,860 less in 30 years of work than a high school graduate. This lack of income causes the government to lose tax dollars. Therefore, the government often has

Chart 2.2 Income by Highest Level of Educational Attainment

Highest level of educational attainment

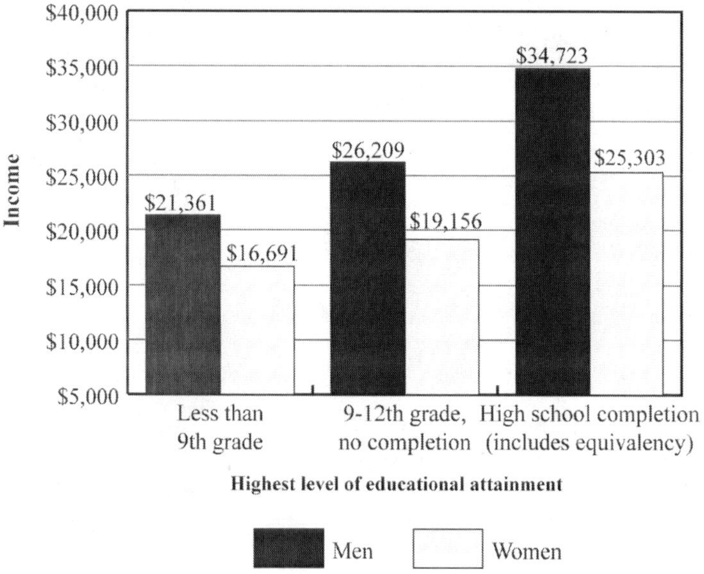

Adapted from U.S. Census, 2005

to pay for social services, such as vocational rehabilitation and low-income health care services.

KINDERGARTEN RETENTION

Every scholar in the field of education, upon reading the reviews of the research literature on grade retention, holds the belief, stated or not, that "None of that research applies to Kindergarten." While it is true that research on retention in grades one to twelve may not apply to kindergartners, there are several dozen studies specifically examining the effects of retention on kindergarten children. The most significant and most sound of these studies are briefly reviewed here. Before reviewing them, however, one must understand the four ways in which young children are retained.

The most obvious way of retention is to have children repeat kindergarten. Another method of retention is to send children to what is often called a "transition room." A transition room is a classroom where children are placed after completing kindergarten, but before they complete first grade. Thus, a transition room is a pre-first-grade room. A third means of retention, oddly enough, is called "red shirting." Red shirting prevents children from entering kindergarten even though they have reached the age of eligibility. The children are simply held out of school until they are six years old. The final means of retention is placing children who are old enough for kindergarten in a pre-kindergarten program. These programs are often called "developmental kindergarten," but the child must still complete a full year of regular kindergarten the following year. Although the means and the nomenclature are different, all four of these approaches result in the same thing: the child entering first grade is at least a year older than their peers.

Unfortunately, researchers have difficulty studying the prevalence of kindergarten retention programs because some states do not keep track of or report the numbers of children retained via the four ways discussed above. One researcher, in 1991, estimated that between one-quarter and one-third of kindergartners are retained nationally. Most researchers, however, have not reported retention rates this high. For example, Peel found that during the 1994–1995 school year, 3,413 kindergartners were retained in the state of North Carolina. This represented 3.5 percent of North Carolina's kindergarten children. In a suburban New York school system of only 3,228 students in grades K–12, 8.6 percent of the entire student population were red shirted or were in a delayed kindergarten-entry program. Of these students, 70 percent were boys and 30 percent were girls. Most research studies investigating early-grade retention have found similar boy-girl differences. Regardless of the wide variety of state-by-state statistics reported by various researchers, it is safe to say that kindergarten retention is widely practiced and that it affects hundreds of thousands of children in the United States each year.

Lorrie Shepard's 1989 review of the research literature on kindergarten retention (via all four methods discussed above) examined 21 studies from the years 1984 to 1989. Here are several of Shepard's conclusions.

WORDS ON FIRE

Kindergarten retention and transition rooms are ineffective. Although a year older than their new grade peers, transition children perform no better academically than transition-eligible children who went directly on to first grade. The finding of no difference or no benefit is true whether children were placed on the basis of pre-academic problems or developmental immaturity. Children who spend an extra year before first grade are just as likely to end up at the bottom of their first or third-grade class as unready children who refused the placement . . . retention, whether it is called by a special name (transition), occurs for special reason (immaturity), or takes place in kindergarten rather than later, is still retention—and still ineffective. (Shepard 1989, 75–76)

To gain additional insight into the reasons why kindergarten teachers retain children, Betty Peel surveyed kindergarten teachers in 565 North Carolina schools (Peel 1997, 146–53). Here are the reasons teachers gave for retaining students and the percentage of times these reasons were given.

Although only 6 percent of the teachers in the study reported "age" as a reason to retain, the researchers found that children who were the youngest were retained the most often. It should also be noted that immaturity (e.g., size of the child) is not a good measure of academic ability. This would be like saying short people are not as smart as tall people.

Table 2.3 Reason Retained	
Academics	56%
Immaturity	50%
Developmental Delays	37%
Home Factors	13%
Exceptional Children	10%
Age	6%
Other	3%
Physical or Health	2%
Adaped from Peel, 1997, p150	

In his 2002 article titled appropriately, "The gift of a year to grow: Blessing or curse," James Gay surveyed the research on early grade retention and had this to say about it:

WORDS ON FIRE

Contrary to "common sense," those pupils given an extra year to grow do less well as measured by future academic success, placement in special education, and persisting through to high school graduation than those children whose parents refuse such practices. (Gay 2002, 63)

REASONS AND MORE REASONS

There are many reasons why retention is simply a bad practice—no matter how well intentioned. The first is simply the cost of retention. In the United States, the cost of educating a single child for one year is approximately $8,000 (NCES, 2005–353). If a student repeats a grade, first grade for example, the cost of one year's worth of education doubles to $16,000. It would be much more cost effective for both the government and the taxpayer to give a qualified teacher $3,000 to give the child one-on-one tutoring. At $30 per hour, you could buy 100 hours of intense remedial instruction. The exact amount each state spends per year to educate a child may be found in table 2.4. It may be of interest to note that the range of per-pupil expenditures goes from a low of $4,838 in Utah to a high of $12,568 in New Jersey.

The second reason why retention is a bad practice is that it makes over-age students. Retained students are at least a year older than their classmates. This is problematic for many reasons throughout the child's school career; however, the problem becomes compounded when a retained student becomes a 19-year-old high school senior. It is even worse for children retained twice because, obviously, they become 20-year-old high school students. When students reach the ages of 19 and 20 years and their age-peers are already out of school, it's tough to persuade them of the benefits of completing high school.

Using a 70-plus-70 analogy, we can outline a third reason why retention is a bad practice. Suppose there is a performance standard of 100 items that first graders need to learn. A child in their first-grade year learns only 70 of the 100 items. If the child is retained, he or she will probably learn the additional 30 things. It is unlikely, however, that the retained child will excel beyond learning first-grade material since the first-grade teacher does not have, and is not expected to teach, second-grade curriculum. If a similar child is promoted and continues to learn merely at the same rate he learned at in the previous year, then the promoted child will have learned 140 things by the end of second grade (70 in first grade and 70 in second grade). This is closely analogous to the research literature that generates a .38 standard-deviation advantage for the promoted child.

A fourth reason why retention is a bad practice comes from a study of the "stressful life events of children." (Yamamoto, Whittaker, and Davis 1998) Over a period of years, Yamamoto and colleagues conducted studies, with nearly identical results, of the stressful life events of children in six cultures. The results reported here are from the United Kingdom study—one of the more recent studies. The researchers asked 366 children ages 7 to 13 years to rate the stressfulness of *potential* life events on a scale from 1 (least stressful) to 7 (most stressful). Table 2.5 shows the results. The table shows that academic retention ranks high on the list of feared potential events. As the researchers explained, "The view of the world seen by a person from the inside

Table 2.4 Annual Cost Per Pupil

State	Per Pupil $	State	Per Pupil $
U.S.	$8,041	Iowa	$7,574
New Jersey	$12,568	California	$7,552
New York	$11,961	Montana	$7,496
Dist. Of Columbia	$11,847	Oregon	$7,491
Connecticut	$11,057	Kansas	$7,454
Massachusetts	$10,460	Colorado	$7,384
Vermont	$10,454	Missouri	$7,349
Rhode Island	$10,349	Washington	$7,252
Alaska	$9,870	Texas	$7,136
Delaware	$9,693	New Mexico	$7,125
Maine	$9,344	South Carolina	$7,040
Maryland	$9,153	Louisiana	$6,922
Wisconsin	$9,004	North Dakota	$6,870
Pennsylvania	$8,997	Kentucky	$6,661
Wyoming	$8,985	North Carolina	$6,562
Michigan	$8,781	South Dakota	$6,547
Ohio	$8,632	Arkansas	$6,482
New Hampshire	$8,579	Florida	$6,439
West Virginia	$8,319	Alabama	$6,300
Illinois	$8,287	Arizona	$6,282
Minnesota	$8,109	Tennessee	$6,118
Hawaii	$8,100	Nevada	$6,092
Nebraska	$8,074	Oklahoma	$6,092
Indiana	$8,057	Idaho	$6,081
Virginia	$7,822	Mississippi	$5,792
Georgia	$7,774	Utah	$4,838

From NCES, 2005-353

Table 2.5 Stressful Life Events

Life event	Mean
Losing parent	6.91
Going blind	6.85
Parental fights	6.57
Caught in theft	6.03
Wetting in class	5.95
Academic retainment	5.71
Suspected of lying	5.13
Having an operation	5.02
A bad report card	4.99
Sent to headteacher	4.96
Ridiculed in class	4.62
Getting lost	4.61
Not good marks in test	4.50
Scary dream	4.00
Move to a new school	3.70
Picked last on team	2.77
Losing in game	2.06
Give class talk	1.98
Going to a dentist	1.31
New baby sibling	1.23
Mean	4.45
Number of children	366.00

Adapted from Yamamoto, Whittaker, & Davis, 1998, p310

does not coincide with the outside-in view held by observers [parents, teachers, and professionals]. For intervention purposes, the inside-out perspective is the more crucial one for us to know, because it largely orients and guides an individual's thoughts, feeling, and actions" (p. 305). The researchers further explained their results as follows:

WORDS ON FIRE

Events perceived the most upsetting by youngsters may be conceptually clustered in two. One is related to the loss of, or threat to, the child's sense of security, exemplified in such events as the loss of a parent (through death, desertion, divorce, separation, mental or physical neglect, long illness, etc.), loss of sight, parental discords, sickness, surgical operation, having a scary dream, displacement (through getting lost physically or mentally, or through relocation, and the like). In a nutshell, most children are very much afraid of being left totally alone. The second cluster has to do with the threat or injury to the child's sense of dignity and respectability. Such experience is revealed in events like being caught in a theft, wetting pants in class, not being promoted to the next grade, being suspected and accused of lying, receiving a bad report card, being sent to the headmaster [principal] for discipline, or being publicly ridiculed. Like everyone else, children fear and detest being shamed and embarrassed. (Yamamoto et al., 311–12)

The problem of boredom provides a fifth reason why retention is a bad practice. In general, teachers within a given grade level teach the same material in the same sequence from year to year. For example, they use the same textbook, and they start at the beginning of that textbook. Thus, a retained child typically starts the whole grade level over again, doing many of the same activities that he or she did the previous year. This leads to boredom and higher incidents of misbehavior and disruption. In stark contrast is the mistaken view that the teacher will individualize instruction for the retained student and start where the child left off last year. In the educational literature, the practice of whole-group instruction has been labeled "teaching to the average student" or "teaching to the middle." Given the ever-increasing number of tasks for which a classroom teacher is responsible, few teachers have the energy, time, or ability to individualize instruction or to tailor instruction to the needs of the retained child.

IN THE WORDS OF DROPOUTS

Although the following information is a bit of a footnote to the above research on retention and dropouts, it is informative to understand one very troubling reality: school officials do follow-up studies on their high school graduates in order to determine what post secondary education they pursue and how they are employed. Ironically, the same school officials rarely do any kind of follow-up studies on their dropouts. Carole Gallagher's 2002 study entitled, "Stories from the Strays: What Dropouts Can Teach Us about Schools, gives us a few insights into what prompts students to quit school and how they reached that decision. Here are the thoughts of the four students Gallagher studied:

WORDS ON FIRE

Dropping out made sense, except for losing my license. This way I could start working more hours in the day. I have a really good job; it's much better than school, for now. [John] Molly added, Things just started sliding too far down-hill. I was wasting my time. It wasn't that big a deal. Chris said, It was a relief. I don't think I could have stood another day. I just got fed up with it; it was the easy way out. When I think of how close I was, I kind of wonder what it would have been like to go ahead and finish. But once you leave, it's over. You can never go back. (p. 44)

When students dropped out of the K–12 school system, they were required to sign a document stating that they understood that they were relinquishing the privilege of being a student, and henceforth they would be prosecuted as a trespasser if caught on school grounds. It is unknown how many school districts in the United States have such a you-can-never-return policy. What is known is that the guidance-counselor-to-pupil ratio in the United States is about one counselor to 500 children. With so few counselors in our high schools, it is unlikely that children contemplating dropping out of school have anyone to talk to about this important decision.

A NOTE TO PARENTS

When it is determined that a practice is harmful, even if it has been used for a long time, it is the duty of practitioners to stop it; it is also the duty of the subjects of the practice to refuse it. I shared a draft of this chapter with a number of noneducators, several of whom had children of their own. The parents in the group all wanted to know what they could do if a school wanted to retain one of their children. Unfortunately, I was unable to give them a solid answer since this varies so much from school district to school district and from state to state. I told the group that they could refuse the placement—a move that *might* work. I say "might" because some states have very rigid laws that basically dictate that a student must pass the state test at a particular grade level or be retained. Still, principals are prone to work with parents. Another option is to get the child some intensive remediation—a topic discussed in chapter 4.

CONCLUSION

Although the means of retaining a child may vary, it is safe to say that retention is, in large part, caused by the fact that children start kindergarten with radically different early-life experiences. Some children come to school far behind their peers in experience and ability. These unfortunate children never catch up and are often retained and are sometimes retained repeatedly. Chapter 3, "Radical Differences in the Early Lives of Children," summarizes the research on these disparities. Additionally, there are a number of proven programs that can be used to help struggling children decrease the learning gap between themselves and their age mates. These catch-up programs are discussed in chapter 4, "Safety Nets, Remedial, and Accelerated Programs."

REFERENCES

Alexander, K.L., D.R. Entwisle, S.L. Dauber, and N. Kabbani. 2004. Dropout in relation to grade retention: An accounting of the Beginning School Study. In H.J. Walberg, H.J., A. J. Reynolds, and M.C. Wang (Eds.) *Can Unlike Students Learn Together? Grade retention, Tracking, and Crowding.* Charlotte, NC: Information Age Publishing: 5–34.

Byrnes, D.A. 1989. Attitudes of students, parents, and educators toward repeating a grade. In L.A. Shepard, and M.L. Smith (Ed.) *Flunking Grades.* New York: Falmer Press: 108–31.

Gallagher, C.J. Summer 2002. Stories from the strays: What dropouts can teach us about school. *American Secondary Education* 30 (3): 36–60.

Gay, J.E. 2002. The gift of a year to grow: Blessing or curse. *Education (Chula Vista, CA)*, 123 (1): 63–72.

Holmes, C.T. 1989. Grade level retention effects: a Meta-analysis of research studies. In L.A. Shepard, and M.L. Smith (Ed.) *Flunking grades.* New York: Falmer Press: 16–33.

Holmes, C.T., and K.M. Matthews. 1984. The Effects of nonpromotion on elementary and junior high school pupils: A meta-analysis. *Review of Educational Research* 54(2): 225–36.

Jimerson, S.R. 2001. Meta-analysis of grade retention research: Implications for practice in the 21st century. *School Psychology Review* 30 (3): 420–37.

Jimerson, S.R. 1999. On the failure of failure: Examining the association between early grade retention and education and employment outcomes during late adolescence. *Journal of School Psychology* 37 (3): 243–72.

Jimerson, S.R., G.E. Anderson, and A.D. Whipple. 2002. Winning the battle and losing the war: Examining the relation between grade retention and dropping out of high school. *Psychology in the Schools* 39 (4): 441–57.

Jimerson, S., E. Carlson, M. Rotert, B. Egeland, and L.A. Sroufe. 1997. A prospective, longitudinal study of the correlates and consequences of early grade retention. *Journal of School Psychology* 35 (1): 3–25.

McCoy, A.R., and A.J. Reynolds. 1999. Grade retention and school performance: An extended investigation. *Journal of School Psychology* 37 (3): 273–98.

Miao, J., and W. Haney. October 15, 2004. High school graduation rates: Alternative methods and implications. *Educational Policy Analysis Archives* 12 (55). Retrieved June 3, 2005 from http://epaa.asu.edu/epaa/v12n55.

NCES (National Center for Education Statistics) Common Core of Data. 2005. *Revenues and expenditures for public elementary and secondary education: School year 2002–2003.* U.S. Department of Education, NCES: 2005–353, 10.

Peel, B.B. 1997. Research vs. practice: Kindergarten retention and student readiness for first grade. *Reading Improvement* 34: 146–53.

Roderick, M.1994. Grade retention and school dropout: Investigating the association. *American Educational Research Journal* 31 (4): 729–59.

Shepard, L.A. 1989. A Review of research on kindergarten retention. In L.A. Shepard, and M.L. Smith (Ed.) *Flunking grades.* New York: Falmer Press: 64–78.

Smith, M.L. 1989. Teachers' beliefs about retention. In L.A. Shepard, M.L. Smith. (Ed.) *Flunking grades.* New York: Falmer Press: 132–50.

U.S. Census Bureau. 2005. Annual demographic survey. Retrieved June, 2006 from http://pubdb3.census.gov/macro/032006/perinc/new01_001.htm.

Walberg, H.J. (2004). Can unlike students learn together? Grade retention, tracking and grouping. Information Age Press.

Yamamoto, K., J. Whittaker, and O.L. Davis. 1998. Stressful events in the lives of UK children: a Glimpse. *Educational Studies* 24 (3): 305–14.

3

Radical Differences in the Early Lives of Children

It is a common misconception among people who have not studied early childhood development that all children come to school equally ready to learn. Sadly, this is definitely not the case, as we will discover in this chapter. While chapter 2 dealt with the problems with the practice of retention, this chapter will illuminate the differences of the children most likely to be retained.

There is copious, and often discouraging, research on child-rearing practices. A single search of the research literature on this topic yielded over 8,000 different articles and studies. The research is dispiriting to read. Sadly, too many families fail to give their children the vital attention necessary for proper development during their critical formative years.

BOOKS IN THE HOME AND SCHOOL

One of the simplest indicators of the radical differences in the early lives of children is the amount of printed material found in the home. In a 1986 study, Feitelson and Goldstein found that "60 percent of the kindergartners in neighborhoods where children tend to do poorly in school did not have a single book. In contrast, kindergartners in neighborhoods where children tend to do well in school owned,

Table 3.1 Average Number of Books in Homes, Classrooms, Schools, and Public Libraries		
Place	Poor Neighborhoods	Affluent Neighborhoods
Home	6	414
Classroom	51	658
School	1,714	11,360
Public Library	50,750	73,000
Adapted from Constantino, 2005, p24		

on average, more than fifty-four books" (Feitelson and Goldstein in Jager-Adams 1995, 88–89).

Research like Feitelson and Goldstein's has been conducted for over 30 years now with remarkably similar results. Rebecca Constantino's 2005 study surveyed sixty students, ranging in age from 7 to 12 years, in each of Los Angeles' six communities. Over a two-year period, the researcher visited the homes of all of these 360 children and simply counted the number of children's books they had in their homes. She also visited their classrooms and counted the number of books there. Dividing her sample between children from affluent neighborhoods and those from poor neighborhoods produced the numbers of books shown in table 3.1. It is interesting to note that the affluent children have more books in their homes than the poor children have in their classrooms. Here are the researcher's conclusions.

WORDS ON FIRE

There is an astonishing difference in access to books among the communities. Not only do children in high SES communities [affluent communities] have more access to books in the home, but also the school does not make up the difference for children in low SES communities [poor communities]. Poor children everywhere are losing out on the opportunity to read and enjoy books, while affluent children are trying to decide what to read next. (Constantino 2005, 24)

READING TO CHILDREN

Since there are so few books in the homes of poor children, it is not surprising that poor children are not being read to nearly as often as their more affluent peers are. Because of this and other factors, by the time poor children enter kindergarten, they are developmentally behind their more-affluent peers and they are less ready to learn, as the following study shows.

In 1998, the National Center for Education Statistics (NCES), a branch of the U.S. Department of Education, began a six-year study, called the "Early Childhood Longitudinal Study," of the nation's children. The study started in the fall of 1998 with an assessment of the kindergartners' readiness for school. Various reports analyzing data from this study, dubbed "ECLS-K," are available on the Web at http://nces.ed.gov/ecls. Findings from this comprehensive study showed substantial inequalities in children's school readiness.

One of the bleak findings of the ECLS-K study is that few poor children are read to on a daily basis by their parents. Chart 3.1 shows the percentage of parents who read to their children daily. The percentage is divided into five income groups, or "quintiles," to use the study's

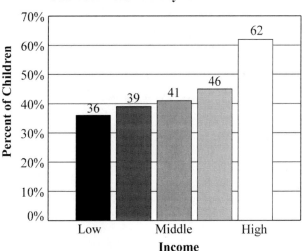

Chart 3.1 Read to Daily: Grade K

Adapted from NCES, 2003

terminology. Notice that 36 percent of the poorest children are read to daily as compared with nearly twice that number or 62 percent of the most-affluent children.

WORDS ON FIRE

To reduce the pervasive inequalities in students' success in school, it is necessary to address the differences that exist among children before they start school. Children come to school with a variety of preschool and home experiences. (Richard J. Coley, *An Uneven Start*, 61–62)

KNOWLEDGE AND SKILLS OF KINDERGARTNERS

Another important finding from the ECLS-K study is that the knowledge and skills children bring to kindergarten varies radically according to the level of education of their mothers. Chart 3.2 shows the reading proficiency of children whose mothers had various levels of education ranging from "less than high school" to holding a "bachelor's degree or higher." Notice that only 38 percent of the children whose mothers had less than a high school diploma could recognize letters. This is in contrast to the 86 percent of the children with mothers who held a bachelor's degree who could recognize letters (ECLS Fall 1998, Table Special 1).

DIFFERENCES IN THE EARLY
LANGUAGE EXPERIENCE OF CHILDREN

Marilyn Jager-Adams, in her landmark book, *Beginning to Read*, describes her son's early language experience.

I estimate that by the time John reaches first grade, we will have spent over 1,000 hours reading to him. (This is thirty to forty-five minutes per day, equaling 180 to 270 hours per year for approximately six years before he enters first grade.) He also will have spent more than 1,000 hours watching *Sesame Street*. And he will have spent a comparable amount of time fooling around with magnetic letters on the refrigerator, writing, participating in reading/writing/language activities at school, playing

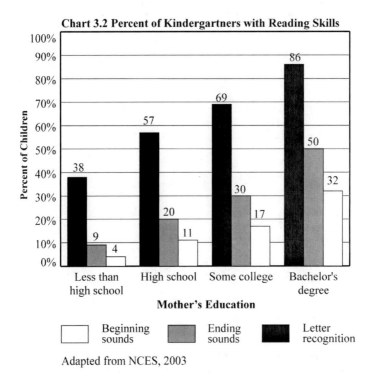

Chart 3.2 Percent of Kindergartners with Reading Skills

Adapted from NCES, 2003

word and spelling games in the car, on the computer, with his sister, and so on. (Jager-Adams 1990, 85)

John, and other fortunate children like him, will enter school with as much as 3,000 hours of early language experience. Many more, however, will not enter school as well prepared to learn to read as John.

To study the early language experience of children, William Teale visited low-income homes in San Diego and counted and timed the literacy activities of 24 preschool children. Across all 24 children, "literacy activities" occurred an average of roughly 10 minutes per day for a total of 60 hours per year. "Story book reading" occurred, on average, less than two minutes per day for a total of only 10 hours per year.

These averages, however, do not show the radically different early language experience of the 24 children Teale studied. Table 3.2 shows

Table 3.2 Story Reading With a Parent: A Study of 24 Children		
	Number of children	Number of occurances
Story Reading	1	26 min. per day
	2	4-5 times a week
	21	5 times a year
Adapted from Teale in Jager-Adams, 1995, p89		

that one child was read to an average of 26 minutes a day, while 21 children were read to only about 5 times in an entire year.

WORDS ON FIRE

Thus it is clear that some children begin school with as much as 3,000 hours of early language experience, while some begin school with as little as 300. (Author)

I was stunned and, quite frankly, heartbroken when I first learned this fact. I asked Marilyn Jager-Adams how this could be. She responded simply, "People who read to their children tend to do so every day. Some people never read to their children. In six years, this adds up." (Personal conversation, University of North Florida, 1995.)

THE ANTIREADING COMMUNITY

In her book *Ways with Words*, Shirley Heath describes a community in which reading is not only *not actively* encouraged, it is *actively discouraged and not valued.* Here is her description of this community.

WORDS ON FIRE

[Reading] was frowned upon, and individuals who did so were accused of being antisocial. Aunt Bertha had a son who as a child used to slip away from the cotton field and read under a tree. He is now a grown man with children, and he has obtained a college degree, but the community still tells tales about his peculiar childhood habits of wanting to go off and read alone. In general,

reading alone, unless one is very old and religious, marks an individual who
cannot make it in society. (Heath 1983)

Educator Jonathon Kozol wrote a book entitled *Savage Inequalities*. I can
think of no better way to summarize the research mentioned earlier.
The obvious question becomes, What is a teacher to do when some
children have 2,700 fewer hours of experience than their classmates?

WORDS IN THE HOMES OF CHILDREN AT AGE 3

The research shows that children enter kindergarten or first grade with
radically different backgrounds and skills. It does not, however, tell
us how early in life good and poor child-rearing practices begin to
have an effect on children. The following landmark research studied
children as they turned three years of age.

Betty Hart and Todd Risley's 1995 book, *Meaningful Differences in
the Everyday Experience of Young American Children*, chronicles their
arduous six-year-long study of the amount and quality of talk that
took place in the homes of 42 children. Hart and Risley's study is so
thorough and informative that it is discussed in detail below.

The researchers made monthly visits to the homes of 42 children.
Thirteen of the 42 children were from professional families, 23 were
from working-class families, and 6 of the children were from welfare
families. Seventeen of the families were African American and 23 of
the children were girls. Once a month for 28 months trained observers went to every one of the 42 homes, where they observed and
audiotaped the interactions between parents and their children. The
observations started when the children were seven to nine months of
age and ended when the children were three years old. In total, the
researchers collected approximately 1,200 hours of audiotape that
was painstakingly transcribed and later coded for computer analysis.
Here are results in the researchers' own words.

WORDS ON FIRE

*The data revealed that, in an average hour together, some parents spent more
than 40 minutes interacting with their child, and other parents spent less than
15 minutes. Some parents responded more than 250 times an hour to their child,
and others responded fewer than 50 times. Some parents expressed approval and*

Table 3.3 Words in the Home by Family Income			
	Welfare	Working-class	Professional
Recorded Vocabulary	974	1498	2176
Utterances per hr.	176	301	487
No. different words/hr	167	251	382
Adapted from Hart & Risley, 1995 in Am. Educator, Spring 2003			

encouragement of their child's actions more than 40 times an hour, and others less than 4 times. Some parents said more than 3,000 words to their child in an average hour together; others said fewer than 500 words. The data showed that the amount the parents talked to their children was so consistent over time that the differences in the child's language experience, mounting up month by month, were enormous by age 3. (Hart and Risley 1995, 128)

Table 3.3 provides a breakdown of the "recorded vocabulary," the "utterances per hour," and the "number of different words used per hour by family type.

Chart 3.3 shows "recorded vocabulary" or total number of words spoken per hour by parents in three different family types.

Perhaps the most damning finding of the Hart and Risley study is that some children grow up in an environment where they are spoken to positively and others grow up in families where they are spoken to negatively. Table 3.4 shows the "affirmations and prohibitions" both per hour and totaled for a one-year period.

The following three pie graphs give a visual picture of the percentage of positive and negative statements heard by the children in these three very different types of families.

As chart 3.4A–C shows, over two-thirds of all the statements heard by the welfare children were negative in tone.

Discussing the cumulative experience of a welfare child in their study, Hart and Risley conclude as follows:

WORDS ON FIRE

The consistency of the data suggests that this child's everyday experience did not greatly differ over the first 3 years. The child's very small net amount of

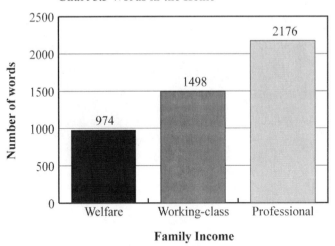

Chart 3.3 Words in the Home

Adapted & Hart and Risley, 1995

Table 3.4 Affirmatives & Prohibitions <u>Per Hour.</u> by Family Type			
	Professional	Working-class	Welfare
Affirmatives	32	12	5
Prohibitions	5	7	11
Affirmatives & Prohibitions <u>Per Year</u>			
	Professional	Working-class	Welfare
Affirmatives	166,000	62,000	26,000
Prohibitions	26,000	36,000	57,000
Adapted from Hart & Risley, 1995 in Am. Educator, Spring 2003			
Note: Data to age 3 yrs.			

Chart 3.4A Professional Families

Prohibitions
14%

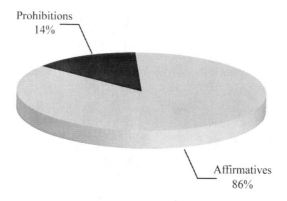

Affirmatives
86%

Adapted from Hart & Risley, 1995

Chart 3.4B Working Class Families

Prohibitions
37%

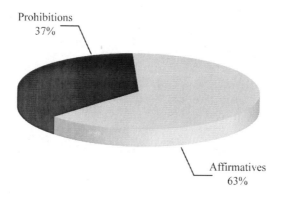

Affirmatives
63%

Adapted from Hart & Risley, 1995

Chart 3.4C Welfare Homes

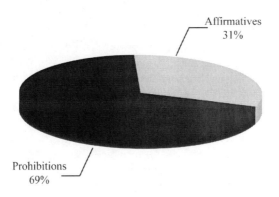

Affirmatives
31%

Prohibitions
69%

Adapted from Hart & Risley, 1995

experience with language [relative to that of the average child] was joined with her proportional experience of being an individual not very "good" and not very interesting to the most important person in her life, the holder of all knowledge and values of the culture. The child was as isolated as her mother was from the sources of knowledge and responses to her skills. We can speculate how much this child will actually know of the world, how it works, and what it contains when she is 3 years old and how capable she will feel competing with her peers in school.

Our experiences in preschool intervention suggest that it will take thousands of hours of affirmative feedback even to begin to overcome what this child has learned about herself in her first 3 years. More thousands of hours will be required to give her the knowledge and vocabulary of even the average children she will meet in school. And this is in the company of those better informed and more confident children that these innumerable experiences of success will have to be arranged. (Hart and Risley 1995, 187–88)

Years ago, the poet Walt Whitman wrote, "Every day a child went forth and everything he looked at he became." The Hart and Risley study could be summarized by saying similarly, "Everyday a child went forth and everything he heard he learned."

BABIES AND BOOKS

This chapter began with a discussion of the radical differences in children at five and six years of age—when they enter kindergarten or first grade. Then differences in children at age 3 were discussed with similar disparities shown. The research literature on children at even younger ages shows similar trends.

Over the last ten years, researchers have been investigating the effects of book reading on infants and toddlers. Bookstart, a "book gifting" project, began in 1992 in Birmingham. Three hundred families who had babies approximately nine months old were given a Bookpack containing a children's book, a bookmark, a poster, and a poem, plus information about library facilities and the value of book sharing and purchase. The investigators found that the families valued the Bookpacks, that they led to positive attitudes toward books, more library enrollments, more book sharing with babies, more book club membership, and subsequently more book purchases (Wade and Moore 1998).

Five years later, when the Bookstart babies entered kindergarten, the researchers conducted a follow-up study of 41 of the original Bookstart babies. The Bookstart children were compared to a matched group of kindergartners who had not participated in the project. The Birmingham schools assess entering kindergartners using six measures—three in reading (speaking and listening, reading, and writing) and three in mathematics (number counting, shapes, and space and measure). Each child's achievement on each of these six assessments was assigned a score from zero to three.

"For reading, there were no scores of 0 for the Bookstart group. About 17 percent of the comparison group scored 0. The only maximum scores of 3 were in the Bookstart group (about 15 percent). Chart 3.5 shows the means for reading of the Bookstart children compared to non-Bookstart group" children (Wade and Moore 1998, 138).

Margaret Hardman and Lynn Jones (1999) reported on a British project similar to Bookstart, called the "Babies into Books" project.

Baby Book Bags, including a free book and other literacy information, were given to 40 caregivers in two targeted areas when their baby was 7 months old, together with an invitation to join a literacy support group called Baby Book Groups. All caregivers were interviewed to assess book-related activity in the home when given the Baby Book Bag. Second interviews two months later with 20 caregivers revealed signifi-

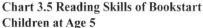

Chart 3.5 Reading Skills of Bookstart Children at Age 5

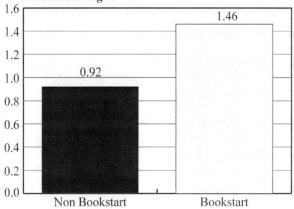

Adapted from Wade & Moore, 1998

cant differences in terms of increases in the number of books owned by the baby, frequency of baby reaching for books and mother and baby looking at children's books and catalogs. These results, and comparison with a control group, confirm the value of this type of early intervention. (Hardman and Jones 1999, 1)

When the babies above were nine months old, the researchers videotaped six mothers involved in the study and five who were not involved. Here is a description of how the Babies into Books mothers and babies interacted with books.

A major feature of the baby's use of books was the way in which it was bounded by physical limitations and lack of mobility. All babies had difficulties in holding the book and moving pages, focusing on images, making intentions known and sitting and righting themselves once they toppled over. They made strong efforts to compensate for their limitations, and we observed the majority using their mouth and several using their feet to hold the book. Physical sensorimotor behaviors included sucking and touching the books in a variety of ways, patting, stroking, scratching, pressing, and flapping the book, looking at the picture on the page and looking at the mother and her actions in relation to the book.

The actions of the mothers facilitated book sharing and included holding the book within the reach of the baby and in its field of focus, moving the baby's hand, pointing at the page, talking about the book, tapping and turning the pages. We observed book-related activities used in a variety of ways; for the learning of motor skills, awareness of the baby's body, control, anticipation, meanings of images, rituals, and social behavior; as well as book reading conventions [for example, reading from front to back of the book]. (Hardman and Jones 1999, 3)

At the beginning of the project, when the babies were seven months old, approximately 10 percent of mothers read to their babies every day. After two months of the project, when the babies were nine months old, over 70 percent of the mothers read to their babies daily.

The researchers concluded that while the mothers appreciated the Baby Book Bag, they also profited from interacting with other mothers and their babies at the Baby Book Group meetings, where they shared their experiences reading to their babies and traded children's books.

The International Reading Association made this strong statement about reading to young children:

WORDS ON FIRE

Failing to give children literacy experiences until they are school age can severely limit the reading and writing levels they ultimately attain. (International Reading Association 1998, 10)

AMERICAN ACADEMY OF PEDIATRICS

Given the above research, it is not surprising that the American Academy of Pediatrics, an organization long known for its strong advocacy, has encouraged early reading through their "Reach Out and Read" (ROR) Program for over 15 years. According to the Academy, children with a "medical home" typically visit their doctor ten times between the age of six months and five years. At each of these visits, children are given a book and are often read to by a volunteer or medical-office worker while they are waiting to see the doctor. In addition, guidance is given to parents or caregivers on literacy activities they can do with their children. In 2004, the ROR program had nearly $10 million in funding from various sources, and it served over two million children in 2,200 clinics in all 50 states (Baily and Rhee 2005). The Academy did not provide statistics on how many children in the United States do not have a "medical home," although that number could well outnumber those who do. Here are a few telling quotes from people involved in, or served by, the ROR program, as reported by Perri Klass in *Pediatrics*, 2002.

> I really enjoy giving the ROR books to the young children. It's actually kind of sad how frequently I hear the parent of a child say, "Wow, a new book—I never got a new book before."—Nurse, Hawaii Health Center

> My kids love to come here and be read to. . . . My children think they are special because their doctor gives them books.—a mother

> I love that the clinic always gives my daughter a book. One time they forgot to give my daughter a book and gave her a sticker and she said, "Wait one minute, where's my book?"—a parent

> My children recently had their physicals, and at that time they were each given a book. . . . That night I believe we read each book four times. It is amazing how much they want me to read to them because the doctor said.—a father

> I am a new father. I'm excited and concerned about being a good father. I was surprised to receive a book for my son at his six-month checkup. I had not thought about reading to him when he is so little.—a father

It is obvious from the above research on reading to infants and toddlers that, by the age of two, some children have had a lot of experience with books and with being read to. Some have not. Unfortunately, there are probably many parents who are like the last father quoted above, parents who have simply never thought about reading to their children when they are infants and toddlers.

POVERTY

Upon reading the reports mentioned earlier, it is impossible not to notice the association between family income and the early lives of children. Obviously, being poor does not make one a bad parent, but it does make it difficult or impossible to provide things like books in the home, health insurance, regular medical checkups, eye glasses, nutritious meals, and adequate housing in anything other than the most run-down neighborhood. Understanding poverty in the United States and its effect on young children is a daunting task for several reasons.

First, to understand poverty, you have to read volumes of information from the United Nations, the World Health Organization, the U.S. Census Bureau, the U.S. Department of Agriculture, the U.S. Department of Education, the U.S. Center for Disease Control, and so on. The second reason why it is difficult to understand poverty is because most of us do not see the poor among us. In the United States, poverty is highly concentrated in certain areas where most of us do not live or travel. Map 3.1 illustrates the concentration of poverty in a large urban area—in this case, Jacksonville, Florida. Third, and perhaps more important, impoverished neighborhoods with substandard housing are unhealthy places to live for many reasons, including high concentrations of lead. (Lead-based paint was banned in 1980.) It would take several book-length volumes to thoroughly cover the effects on children of being poor, so the coverage below only briefly outlines the problem.

In a wealthy nation such as the United States of America, you would think that poverty would not be a problem. After all, we offer free or reduced-price breakfast and lunch to the poor, we give poor children free vision-screening in school, and so on. The data, however, show a much different reality.

Chart 3.6 shows the most recent UNICEF childhood poverty rates in 26 of the world's richest countries. According to UNICEF, 22 percent of U.S. children live in poverty, and we are 25th out of 26 nations—just slightly ahead of Mexico (UNICEF 2005, 6).

Table 3.5 summarizes information on U.S. children living in poverty from two sources: UNICEF and the U.S. Census Bureau. Notice that the two sources provide similar data.

It is disheartening to further report that the median annual income in the United States varies radically by race as shown in table 3.6 (U.S. Census Bureau 2004, 4).

In his 2005 presidential address to the American Educational Research Association's annual meeting, renowned researcher David Berliner offered this description of the effect of poverty on children and schools.

Poverty in Duval County Florida, 2000

**Percentage of Population
Below Poverty Level**

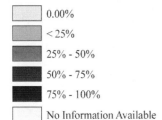

0.00%
< 25%
25% - 50%
50% - 75%
75% - 100%
No Information Available

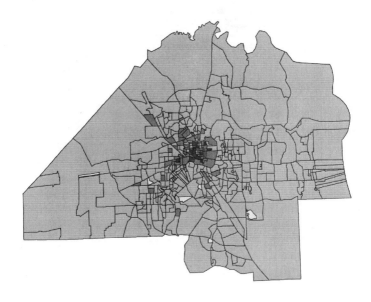

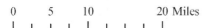

0   5   10   20 Miles

From U.S. Census data 2000

Chart 3.6 UNICEF Child Poverty Rates, 2005

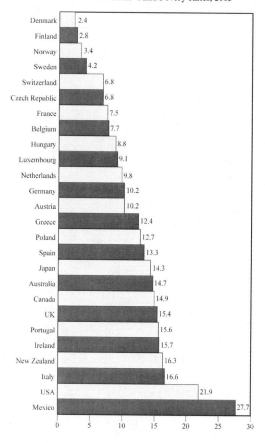

Adapted from UNICEF, 2005

WORDS ON FIRE

Policy makers almost universally conclude that existing and persistent achievement gaps must be the result of wrongly designed school policies—either expectations are too low, teachers are insufficiently qualified, curricula are badly designed, classes are too large, school climates are too undisciplined, leadership that is unfocused, or a combination of these.

Americans have concluded that the achievement gap is the fault of "failing schools" because it makes no common sense that it would be otherwise. This

Table 3.5 Income, Poverty, and Health Insurance Coverage for Children 18 Years Old and Younger

	UNICEF	U.S. Census
Poverty Level	$22,000	$19,157
Children in poverty	22%	17.80%
Number in poverty	10 million	13 million
No health insurance		11.20%
No health insurance		8.3 million

UNICEF, 2005, p6, and U.S. Census Bureau, 2005, p9, 16

Table 3.6 Median Annual Income in the U. S. By Race, 2004

Asian	$57,196
White	$46,857
Hispanic	$33,884
Black	$30,442

U. S. Census Bureau, 2004, p4

common sense perspective, however, is misleading and dangerous. It ignores how the social class characteristics in a stratified society like ours may actually influence learning in schools. (pp. 9–10)

For nearly half a century, the association of social and economic disadvantage with a student achievement gap has been well known by economists, sociologists, and educators. Most, however, have avoided the obvious implication of this understanding— raising the achievement of lower-class children requires the amelioration of the social and economic conditions of their lives, not just school reform. (p. 11)

FOOD INSECURITY AND HUNGER

One of the difficulties poor families have is feeding their children. Again, in a developed country like the United States, one would not think that hunger would be a problem, but for a portion of the population, it is. The United States Department of Agriculture (USDA) defines households with "food security" as those that "... had access at all times [during a year] to enough food for an active, healthy life for all household members" (Nord, Andrews, and Carlson, 2004, 1). In 2004, 87 percent of American households were food secure, 13 percent were food insecure. Here are a few facts from the USDA.

- 13 percent of U.S. households were food insecure in 2004.
- 24.3 million adults and 13.9 million children lived in food-insecure households.
- 7.4 million adults and 3.3 million children lived in households where someone experienced hunger during the year.
- 545,000 children experienced hunger in 2004.
- Food-secure households spent 31 percent more on food than did food-insecure households.
- About half of food-insecure households participated in a federal food-assistance program (Nord, Andrews, and Carlson, 2004, 16).

Most adults in "food-insecure households with hunger" go hungry themselves before making their children go hungry. This accounts for the low number of children, 545,000, who were hungry in 2004. The data do not describe the effect that having a hungry parent might have on a child.

COST OF FOOD AND HEALTH CARE

Table 3.7 shows the difference between food and health care spending of the poorest and richest households. Notice that the richest families spend nearly three times more on food than do the poorest families.

Table 3.8 shows the USDA's estimates of the amount of money needed to feed a family of four with two preschool children. Notice that the amount of money spent on food by the poorest families, $3,178, is substantially less that what the USDA estimates is required on the "thrifty food plan," which is $5,070. That is to say, the

Table 3.7 Expenditures for Food and Healthcare of the Poorest and Richest Families

Average Income	Spent on food	Percent of income	Spent on healthcare	Percent of income
$18,492	$3,178	17	$1,439	8
$81,731	$9,039	11	$3,606	4

Adapted from USDA, 2005, table 13

Table 3.8 USDA Cost of Food – Thrifty & Low-cost Plans for a Family of Four

	Weekly	Yearly
Thrifty plan	$97.50	$5,070.00
Low-cost plan	$122.50	$6,370.00

USDA Center for Nutrition Policy and Promotion, February 2004

poorest families spend nearly $2,000 less on food than the USDA estimates it takes to feed their families nutritious meals. It is probably also true that following the thrifty food plan would take some very careful shopping.

LEAD POISONING IN CHILDREN

Because poor children are likely to live in older, inner-city neighborhoods, they often live in older homes that were painted with lead-based paint. In addition, older intercity neighborhoods are often traversed or bordered by multilane freeways. Before the advent of unleaded gasoline, the traffic on these freeways deposited heavy concentrations of lead particulates on the soil in these neighborhoods. Unfortunately, lead is highly toxic, especially to children under six years of age. There is some disagreement about how high the concentration of lead in the body has to be before it is injurious—some experts claim that any level has an ill effect. According to the U.S. Center for Disease Control (CDC),

> Lead is a soft, heavy, blue gray metal. It occurs naturally in the Earth's crust, and human activities such as burning fossil fuels, mining, and manufacturing have spread it throughout the environment, including our homes and workplaces.
>
> Exposure to lead should be avoided. Lead is highly toxic to humans, especially to young children. It has no known physiologic value to the human body. Nearly half a million children living in the United States have enough lead in their blood to cause irreversible [neurological] damage to their health.
>
> Data from [a major national study] showed that low-income children living in older housing had more than a 30-fold greater prevalence of [high levels of lead in their blood] than do middle-income children in newer housing. (CDC: Lead: Questions and Answers, http://www.cdc.gov)

Many education writers dispute the CDC's estimate of the number of children with lead poisoning, believing it is, in reality, much higher. They base their reasoning on the large number of children living in poverty in older homes. They also argue that the CDC's "Blood Lead Level" threshold is set too high.

Bailus Walter, dean of the Public Health School at the University of Oklahoma, had this to say about lead poisoning in children (Walter 2005).

WORDS ON FIRE

The education community has not really understood the dimensions of this because we don't see kids falling over and dying of lead poisoning in the classroom. But there's a very large number of kids who find it difficult to do analytical work or [even] line up in the cafeteria because their brains are laden with lead. (Walter and Berliner 2005)

According to the U.S. National Institute of Health, "There are many possible symptoms of lead poisoning. Lead can affect many different parts of the body. Over time, even low levels of lead exposure can harm a child's mental development. The possible health problems get worse as the level of lead in the blood gets higher" (http://www.nlm .nih.gov/medlineplus/ency/article/002473.htm).

Possible complications of lead poisoning

- Reduced IQ
- Slowed body growth
- Hearing problems
- Behavior or attention problems
- Failure at school
- Kidney damage

The symptoms of lead poisoning may include

- Irritability
- Aggressive behavior
- Low appetite and energy
- Difficulty sleeping
- Headaches
- Reduced sensations
- Loss of previous developmental skills (in young children)
- Anemia
- Constipation
- Abdominal pain and cramping (usually the first sign of a high, toxic dose of lead poisoning)
- Very high levels may cause vomiting, staggering gait, muscle weakness, seizures, or coma.

AT-RISK CHILDREN

The education science discussed in this chapter makes it clear that many children are at risk of academic failure; that is only one risk factor affecting children. Jack Frymier's large-scale study of factors affecting children identified five risk categories: academic failure, family instability, family socioeconomic situation (income), family tragedy, and personal pain (e.g., the child was abused or attempted suicide). Here is Frymier's poignant conclusion to the study.

WORDS ON FIRE

*A student at risk in one area is very likely to be at risk in many other areas.
Risk is pervasive. Children who hurt, hurt all over. Children who fail, often fail
at everything they do.* (Frymier 1992)

CONCLUSION

When taking into consideration the early lives of children, it is necessary to consult many sources of information like those reviewed in
this chapter. Simply considering the early language development, or
early learning, of children would give an incomplete picture of how
radically different their lives can be. When these children with radical
differences enter school, they are either ignored or accommodated.
When these differences are ignored, they contribute significantly
to the grade retention problem discussed in chapter 2. In the next
chapter, "Safety Nets and Remedial Programs," we will review the
interventions that have and have not been successful in helping low-
performing children catch up to their peers.

REFERENCES

Bailey, R., and K.B.L. Rhee. 2005. Reach out and read: Promoting pediatric
literacy guidance through a transdisciplinary team. *Journal of Health Care for
the Poor and Underserved* 16 (2): 225–30.

Coley, R.J. March, 2002. *An uneven start: Indicators of inequality in school readiness*. Princeton, New Jersey: Educational Testing Service.

Constantino, R. February 2005. Print environments: Between high and low
socioeconomic status (SES) communities. *Teacher Librarian* 32 (3).

ECLS. Early Childhood Longitudinal Study. National Center for Educational
Statistics, *The Condition of Education*, 2003, Early Literacy Activities, Indicator 37, NCES 2003–067, 164–65.

Frymier, J. (November, 1992). Children who hurt. Children who fail. Phi
Delta Kappan, 257.

Hardman, M., and L. Jones. 1999. Sharing books with babies: Evaluation of
an early literacy intervention. *Educational Review* 51 (3): 221–30.

Hart, B., and T.R. Risley. 1995. *Meaningful differences in the everyday experience of
young American children*. Baltimore, Maryland: Paul H. Brooks Publishing.

Heath, S.B. 1983. *Ways with words*. Cambridge: Cambridge University Press.

International Reading Association/National Association for the Education of Young Children. 1998. Learning to read and write: Developmentally appropriate practices for young children. *The Reading Teacher* 52: 193–216.

Jager-Adams, M. 1995. *Beginning to read.* Cambridge, Massachusetts: MIT Press.

Justice, L.M., and P.C. Pullen. 2003. Promising interventions for promoting emergent literacy skills: Three evidence-based approaches. *Topics in Early Childhood Special Education* 23 (3): 99.

Klass, P. 2002. Pediatrics by the book: Pediatricians and literacy promotion. *Pediatrics* 110 (5): 989–96.

Linebarger, D.L. 2001. Beginning literacy with language: Young children learning at home and school. *Topics in Early Childhood Special Education* 21 (3): 188.

Neuman, S.B., and D. Celano. 2001. Books aloud: A campaign to "put books in children's hands." *The Reading Teacher* 54 (6): 550.

(NCES) National Center for Education Statistics. 2003. *The condition of education 2003: Indicator 37: Early literacy activities.* United States Department of Education, Institute of Education Statistics. NCES: 2003–67.

Nord, M., M. Andrews, and S. Carlson. 2004. *Household food security in the United States, 2004.* United States Department of Agriculture, Economic Research Service, 2004/ERR-11.

UNICEF 2005. *Child poverty in rich countries: 2005. Innocenti Research Report Card No. 6.* Florence, Italy: Innocenti Research Center.

USDA, United States Department of Agriculture, Assistance and Nutrition Research Report No. (FANRR19-4) 174 pp., December 2004.

Wade, B., and M. Moore. 1998. An early start with books: Literacy and mathematical evidence from a longitudinal study. *Educational Review* 50 (2): 135.

Walter, B. in D.C. Berliner (August 2005). Our impoverished view of educational reform. *Teachers College Record.* New York: Columbia University.

4

Safety Nets and Remedial Programs

Given the radical differences in the early lives of the children discussed in chapter 3, the obvious question is, what can be done to help? A careful reader of chapter 3 would notice that many problems are caused by poverty, substandard living conditions, poor parenting skills, and the like. These problems need to be addressed by policymakers and government leaders since they are largely not the purview of educators. Schools cannot fix all the problems of a society. A careful reader of chapter 3 is also likely to conclude that some of the solutions are obvious. For example, if poor children have few books, then devise ways to give them books.

The discussion in this chapter will focus on preventative programs—often called "safety nets"—that try to help children before they get behind and on remedial programs aimed at helping children who are already behind their peers. Both reading and language arts programs as well as math programs will be reviewed. The discussion will *not* deal with effectively teaching the approximately 80 percent of the children who are functioning at or near grade level. Obviously, children who fall far behind their classmates are a great challenge for teachers and schools.

BOOKS ALOUD

In 2001, Susan Neuman and Donna Celano reported on the results of a two-year program, called "Books Aloud," that put high-quality children's books in urban child-care centers in the Delaware Valley region of Pennsylvania. The project was a collaborative effort between the Office of Public Service Support of the Free Library of Philadelphia and seven county and city library systems. "Books Aloud was designed to enrich the lives of economically disadvantaged children in child-care centers and support the child-care givers who sheltered those toddlers and preschoolers through long days that stretch from before dawn to past supper time." Dick Cox, the vice president of the local foundation that helped fund the project said, "We knew that these children often spent more waking hours at child-care centers than they do at home" (Neuman and Celano 2001, 551).

Books Aloud "provided more than 89,000 brand-new story books to 17,675 toddlers and preschoolers in child-care centers and family child-care homes, along with book cases and storage and display racks to create library corners in classrooms. In a single month, 325 child-care centers and 250 family child-care homes—at a ratio of five books per child—were flooded with sturdy board books, beautiful picture books, and books that rhymed and counted and told wonderful stories." Books Aloud even promised to help ". . . repair the books after they'd been played with and ripped and loved to the point of falling apart" (p. 51).

Books Aloud went beyond just flooding child-care facilities with books, they also provided 10 hours of training for the child-care providers. "The purpose of the training program was to emphasize the importance of the early years in establishing a foundation for literacy, to create environments that engage children in print activities, to foster effective read-aloud techniques, and to make story reading a constant presence in their everyday activities—not just a 'fill-in' activity wedged between arts and crafts and nap time" (p. 551).

Results of the project demonstrated that, when compared to their counterparts, Books Aloud children were dramatically ahead in awareness of letter-sound connections, letter knowledge, narrative abilities, and writing. Here is the researchers' conclusion.

WORDS ON FIRE

Therefore, given the enormous disparities among different income groups, how can we ensure that all children have an equal opportunity to succeed in reading? As we confirmed in this research, increase the volume, quality, and intensity of young children's stimulating experience with good books at an early age. (p. 557)

Programs like Books Aloud and the ROR program of the American Academy of Pediatric Physicians, which were discussed in chapter 3 and which enrich the print environment of young children, are viable ways to help disadvantaged children enter school more able to keep up with their peers.

READING RECOVERY

Reading Recovery (RR) is an early intervention program designed to help low-achieving first graders who are in the lowest quartile of performance. RR was developed 25 years ago by New Zealand educator and psychologist Marie Clay. The program is now widely used in nearly all U.S. states, Canada, England, New Zealand, and Australia. "By 2001–2002, about 18,000 trained teachers offered RR to over 146,000 students in 10,451 schools located in 3,238 school districts nationwide [in the U.S.]" (Gemoz-Bellenge, in D'Agostino and Murphy, 24).

RR teachers go through an entire year of intensive professional development usually provided by a university center licensed by the Reading Recovery Council of North America, which is housed at the Ohio State University. Children in the program receive 30 minutes of daily one-on-one instruction for up to 20 weeks. "RR instruction has the following characteristics:

- Teachers focus on each student's strengths, not deficits;
- Students learn strategies that help them to become independent readers;
- Students learn to read by composing and writing their own messages;
- Teachers base instruction on detailed analysis of student behavior and knowledge;

- Students are taught how to predict, confirm, and understand what they have read; and
- Teachers can select student reading materials from over 2,000 small books of increasing difficulty (U.S. DOE 1992, 1).

A typical RR lesson might proceed as follows:

1. The child rereads several familiar books.
2. The child rereads a book introduced in the prior lesson while the teacher does a running record (observes and records the child's reading behavior). The teacher chooses 2–3 powerful teaching points.
3. The child is guided toward discovering how words work through developing letter knowledge and word structure awareness and familiarity.
4. The child writes a story with the teacher providing opportunities for him/her to hear and record sounds in words.
5. The child rearranges his/her story from a cut-up sentence strip provided by the teacher.
6. The teacher introduces a new book carefully selected for its learning opportunities.
7. The child reads the new book orchestrating his/her current problem-solving strategies (Conneautville School District, Retrieved from the Internet, April 4, 2006).

According to Reading Recovery Council of North America, the criteria for a child's successful completion of the program includes the ability to read texts that have

- long stretches of print with few pictures,
- full pages of print without pictures,
- complex story structures that require sophisticated ways of understanding,
- complex ideas that require background knowledge to understand and interpret,
- many multisyllable words,
- new words to decode without help from illustrations, and
- some vocabulary words that are unfamiliar.

META-ANALYSIS OF READING RECOVERY—36 STUDIES

In 2004, Jerome D'Agostino and Judith Murphy published their meta-analysis of 36 studies of the effectiveness of RR. The researchers examined a total of 109 studies but rejected all but 36 for appropriate technical reasons. Most RR students in the various studies were selected from children who scored below the 20th percentile. The overall effect size across 36 studies was .27 in favor of students who had discontinued the program, i.e., graduated from RR. Here are the researchers' conclusions.

WORDS ON FIRE

On posttest standardized achievement measures, discontinued students [who had completed RR] significantly outperformed similar needy but not "regular" students. Discontinued students outperformed "regular" students on three Observation Survey measures (Writing Vocabulary, Hearing and Recording Sounds in Words, and Text Reading Level) and outperformed similar needy students on six Observation Survey Tests. At a 2nd grade follow-up [a year later], discontinued and all treatments students combined outperformed their similar needy peers on Standardized Achievement Tests [e.g., Comprehensive Test of Basic Skills and Iowa Test of Basic Skills]. (D'Agostino and Murphy 2004, 31–32)

Admittedly RR is an expensive program, which costs approximately $7,000 per student served. Dyer (1992) argued persuasively that RR is in fact cost effective due to "(1) not having to retain low-achieving students in first grade; (2) not having to place students in special education or chapter 1 programs; and (3) not mislabeling a child as 'learning disabled' when in fact the child needed only brief, supplementary intervention provided by Reading Recovery."

Although RR is a one-on-one intervention, recent research indicates that it may be possible to place two or even three students with a single RR teacher. Official RR policy statements argue against such a practice.

READING RECOVERY WITH PAIRS OF STUDENTS

To investigate the effect of placing two students at a time in RR, Sandra Iverson, William Tunmer, and James Chapman (2005) conducted a pilot study and a well-controlled, experimental study to compare one-on-one instruction and two-on-one instruction. Seventy-five of the lowest performing first-grade students in a rural southern school district participated in the study. The children who were taught individually and in pairs each received 60 RR lessons. Here is the researcher's conclusion.

WORDS ON FIRE

The results of the experimental study indicated that although RR instruction in pairs required somewhat longer lessons (42 min vs. 33 min) there were no major differences between the two experimental groups on any measure at discontinuation and at the end of the year, nor was there a significance between the groups in the mean number of lessons to discontinuation. The results further indicate that by discontinuation, the children in the treatment groups were performing within the average range on all measures and that these positive effects maintained at the end-of-year measures. In summary, the results suggest that the same outcomes of RR can be achieved by struggling readers taught in pairs as by those taught individually by increasing the duration of the lesson an average of only 9 min. Thus by increasing instructional time about a quarter, RR teachers can double the number of students served without making any sacrifice in outcomes (Iverson, Tunmer, and Chapman 2005, 470–71).

EARLY STEPS READING

Early Steps, developed by Darrell Morris (Morris, Shaw, and Penny 1990; Santa 1998), is a little-known, early-intervention program, for at-risk first graders that is similar to RR. A major difference between the two programs is that RR teachers are in training full time for an entire year. Early Steps teachers can be trained in professional development sessions and/or in an on-campus graduate course. This makes Early Steps substantially less expensive to implement since an entire group of teachers can be trained for about the cost of training a single RR teacher. Another difference is that Early Steps puts more emphasis on phonemic awareness, which is the association between letters and sounds. Here is an example of an Early Steps activity called "word sorting." Children are given 9 to 12 words and are asked to put them in the appropriate category. Here is an example.

bat	man	cap
rat	fan	map
cat	pan	lap
sat	can	tap

After children can easily sort words like those above, they move on to recognizing patterns in words such as consonant-vowel-consonant. Here is an example (Santa and Hoien 1999, 63).

can	pig	hot
hat	sit	top
lap	in	job
bag	lip	stop

The 30-minute Early Steps lessons had four parts: rereading familiar books, word study, writing, and introduction of a new book. Both RR and Early Steps make use of "leveled books," which are carefully sequenced into small increments of increasing difficulty.

In 1999, Santa and Hoien reported the results of a yearlong study of the effectiveness of Early Steps that was conducted in four neighborhood schools in Kalispell, Montana. All four first-grade teachers, four Title One teachers, a language arts coordinator, and a principal participated in the study. Forty-nine of the lowest performing first-grade students (bottom 20 percent of the class) from the four classrooms were selected to be in the study and were randomly placed in the "treatment group" (23 children) and a control/comparison group (26 children). Half of the teachers were assigned to the treatment group; half were assigned to the control group. Children in the treatment group received 30 minutes of one-on-one reading instruction that followed the Early Steps model. The control group children attended their regular Title One reading classes. Early Steps teachers tutored their students during their planning period. In some cases, a paraprofessional or a parent read to a class while the Early Steps teacher tutored children. Table 4.1 shows the results of the study.

Here are the researchers' conclusions.

WORDS ON FIRE

In summary, the experimental [treatment] group statistically [and] significantly outperformed the control group on all post-intervention tests.

Table 4.1 Early Steps Reading – Study Results		
Posttest	Treatment avg.	Control avg.
Passage reading	21.3	16.3
Word identification	39.1	33.6
Word attack skills	20.5	12.7
Adapted from Santa & Hoien, 1999, p67		

Our data clearly show that Early Steps led to accelerated growth, particularly for children most at risk for not learning to read. Moreover, these results were substantiated on a variety of dependent measures and were maintained over the summer after students had completed the program. (Santa and Hoien 1999, 67 and 69)

According to the researchers, Early Steps works because "It represents a balanced program that incorporates key features of effective reading instruction. It takes place early, before children develop ineffective habits and devastating psychological problems about their learning inadequacies. It also provides children with the opportunity to make accelerated progress. Children spend time reading books rather than with fragmented texts and isolated drills. The time spent reading is with books that match the child's instructional level. Students also progress through levels of books that become progressively more difficult (Santa and Hoien 1999, 72).

Obviously, it is easier to catch poor readers when they are young, before their problems multiply. By the third or fourth grade, poor readers may be as much as two or more years behind their classmates. The next research discussed focuses on helping intermediate grade students (grades 3 to 6).

RESISTANT OR RELUCTANT READERS

If students develop a dislike for reading, they resist reading and some even hate reading. In the research literature, these children are labeled either "resistant" or "reluctant" readers. One-on-one reading programs like RR and Early Steps are primarily offered in first- or second-grade classrooms and are rarely if ever considered options for students in grades three to six. This is probably because of the high cost of such programs.

WORDS ON FIRE

When I was a little girl I loved to read. I mean I was so smart. I was excellent. I was reading the newspaper when I was eight. When I was a little girl I would just read and read every night. I would read a whole book every night. I'd read one page and mom would read one page. . . . But then when I got older I got interested in a lot of other things and I just put that aside and I started forgetting how to read. . . . When I got older, I just hated to read. (Marta, a fifth grader in Worthy and others, 2002, 177)

Research on remedial reading instruction in the intermediate grades tends to focus on attributes of successful interventions rather than on comprehensive programs like RR. Here are a few of the characteristics of successful reading programs for reluctant readers.

META-ANALYSIS OF REPEATED READING

Reading the same short and meaningful passages three or four times aloud to an adult was shown by William Therrien in a meta-analysis to be extremely helpful in increasing reading fluency and comprehension. Fluency is basically defined as reading faster with fewer errors. Therrien found a mean effect size, across 16 studies that measured fluency, of .50. Repeated reading to an adult increased student fluency half a standard deviation. The researcher found a mean effect size, across 11 studies that measured comprehension, of .25. Thus, repeated reading to an adult increased student comprehension a fourth of a standard deviation. Therrien also found that reading aloud to adults was substantially more effective than reading aloud to a peer or to an older student. Other factors that helped increase fluency and comprehension were modeling of reading by an adult and offering corrective feedback to students when they asked for help—for example, in pronouncing an unfamiliar word (Therrien 2004, 3). Given these results, it is easy to see why both RR and Early Steps programs make heavy use of the repeated-reading strategy.

INTEREST AND ACCESS

Teachers and parents of reluctant readers often find that even though they have large collections of children's books and magazines, students often complain of not having anything interesting to read. The research literature points to the importance of finding just the right hook to get reluctant readers interested in reading. Reading-interest inventories have been devised to help (McKeena and Robinson 2002). Both anecdotal data and numerous research studies report on a varied and sundry array of print material that various teachers and researchers have used to get reluctant students to read including

- Comic books
- Newspapers
- Magazines, e.g., *Boys Life, Girls Life, National Geographic Explorer, Hot Rod, Teen People,* and *Sports Illustrated*
- *Guinness Book of World Records*
- Extreme sports magazines and books
- Chapter books
- Joke books
- Riddles

Obviously, reading anything is better than reading nothing.

THE HUMAN FACTOR IN HELPING RELUCTANT READERS

Many years ago, researchers investigating different approaches to one-on-one psychological counseling found that the intent of the counselor to help was more important than any specific counseling technique or practice. Counselors with a deep desire to help their clients worked until they found a way to do so. This intent to help also applies to tutors of reluctant readers.

Jo Worthy and others reported on a study of 24 reluctant or resistant readers in grades 3 through 5. The study took place in an elementary school in a large urban school district in the southwestern United States. The researchers tutored children one-on-one in the "reading club," an after-school literacy tutorial program. The 24 reluctant readers were tutored by five university researchers with teaching experience, ten graduate students in a "reading difficulties class," and 16 preservice teachers in a reading-methods class. Children were tutored twice a week for one semester or more.

The tutoring program included many elements discussed previously including "fluent and supported reading instruction, word study, writing a response to reading, and read aloud, reader's theater, and book discussion" (Worthy et al. 2002, 184).

Using their personal libraries of children's books, donations, and a grant from the state education agency, the researchers were able to assemble a collection of 3,000 books and other reading material. The tutors used this extensive collection of resources housed in the "reading club" classroom to individualize their work with the children.

> Finding a topic of interest, in fact, was rarely a problem even for the most resistant readers. Finding materials, however, that were high quality, appropriately challenging, and up-to-date about subjects of interest and relevance was a constant challenge. These students needed an intermediary, the tutor, to help them find such reading material. Some students' interests were unusual enough that tutors had to look beyond typical schoolbook sources. Even the reading club library, which included many unconventional materials, was no match for students who initially wouldn't look at any books and only were interested in topics such as wrestling, popular musicians and actors, low rider bikes, video games, and the army. (Worthy et al., 189)

WORDS ON FIRE

> *When they [students] found success with an easy book during tutoring, many students would not take them out of the reading club. Don, a 4th grader, explained that although he loved Dr. Seuss books, he wouldn't check them out of the library because, "I don't want my friends to laugh at me.* (Worthy et al., 189)

Twenty-one of the 24 students in the reading club greatly increased their at-home voluntary reading. The mean increase in voluntary reading was from less than one short book or chapter per week to five short books or chapters per week. In addition, each student increased their reading achievement by a minimum of one grade level and a maximum of five grade levels, with an average of one grade level or progress per semester.

WORDS ON FIRE

As previous research has suggested, social interaction, students' interests, and access to appropriate texts were all key factors in promoting voluntary reading for resistant readers in our study. Our findings suggest that while these factors were each necessary, their influence was different for each student and could even be negative. Even together they were not sufficient to turn most of the resistant readers into interested readers for whom reading was a voluntary activity. In case after case of students who overcame their reading resistance, the factor that was the most salient was the human factor, the tutor who took personal responsibility for the student. (p. 188)

Many tutors went well beyond these requirements [expectations] making frequent contacts with their child's family through calling, walking their students home after tutoring, and making home visits. Some took their students on trips to the bookstore or public library or on other outings. When students were not reading at home, many tutors took the responsibility to call the students' families and collaborate on how to improve the situation. (p. 193)

Given the research discussed so far, it seems obvious that once a child gets behind their peers in reading and becomes a reluctant or resistant reader, it takes a large amount of effort to remediate the student. Given the research, it also seems obvious that we have the knowledge, techniques, and skills to help struggling readers. The effort required to make a difference, however, is substantial.

REMEDIAL MATHEMATICS

One-on-one intervention programs for struggling mathematics students are uncommon, and there is no definitive body of education science on such programs. There is, however, ample education science that can be used to guide practitioners who want to help struggling mathematics students.

MATHEMATICS INTERVENTIONS FOR CHILDREN WITH SPECIAL NEEDS A META-ANALYSIS—58 STUDIES

Evelyn Kroesbergen and Johannes Van Luit (2003), two researchers in the Netherlands, did a meta-analysis of 58 studies conducted

Table 4.2 Mathematics Intervention – Basic Facts	
Intervention	Effect Size
Peer Tutoring	-0.76
Self instruction	0.76
Direct instruction	1.55
Adapted from Kroesbergen & Van Luit, 2003, p3	

with special-education students. There were a total of 2,509 children in the studies—all had special needs in the area of math. The studies were grouped in two different ways: by type of instruction/intervention and by math content. Table 4.2 shows the effect size by type of instruction on basic facts. Notice the negative effect size for peer tutoring. Peer tutoring is often advocated as an effective instructional technique by educators interested in educational innovations. The research on instruction, however, clearly demonstrates the superiority of a qualified teacher working directly with children on the content of the lesson.

The researchers also examined the use of computer-assisted instruction (CAI), which showed a weak but positive effect, but there was a small number of studies that used CAI, so it is not included in table 4.2. The meta-analysis also considered interventions in "preparatory mathematics" (e.g., serial ordering), but this content area was not abundant in the studies reviewed. The researchers' conclusions are presented here.

WORDS ON FIRE

When choosing and organizing an intervention, one should keep in mind the following findings. The first finding concerns the method used to teach students mathematics. Both self-instruction and direct instruction seem to be adequate methods for students with special needs.

The results of the present study show that in general, traditional interventions with humans as teachers, and not computers, are most effective.

We often have children work together in order that they might teach each other. It appears, however, that children with special needs do not particularly profit from this strategy.

Finally, this study suggests that not all changes proposed by math reformers are as effective as more traditional approaches. (Kroesbergen and Van Luit 2003, 113)

EMPIRICAL RESEARCH ON TEACHING
MATHEMATICS TO LOW-ACHIEVING STUDENTS
A META-ANALYSIS—15 STUDIES

In science, the most rigorous research is experimental and quasi-experimental. In experimental research, subjects are randomly sampled from a large population and are randomly placed into two groups: an experimental or treatment group and a control or comparison group. Quasi-experimental research is similar, except that classrooms of children are randomly placed into experimental and control groups. The ·following meta-analysis was limited to studies using experimental and quasi-experimental research.

Scott Baker, Russell Gersten, and Dae-Sik Lee (2002) did a meta-analysis of 15 studies in an effort to synthesize research on the effects of interventions to improve math achievement of low-achieving students. A major strength of this meta-analysis is that all of the studies were scientifically rigorous, and they used reliable and valid outcome measures of math achievement. The 15 studies in the synthesis were carefully selected from more than 194 initial studies. Table 4.3 presents the results of the meta-analysis.

It is important to note that the peer-assisted learning-intervention effect size of .66 is for computation (basic math facts) only. This finding is in stark contrast to the effect size of –.76 in the meta-analysis described earlier, which was done with special-education students. Perhaps special students are less able to help their peers. Here are the researchers' overall conclusions: "Providing teachers and students with specific information on how each student is performing seems to enhance mathematics achievement. The practice has been recommended for many years, yet the extent to which it is implemented is unclear. The effect of such practice is substantial."

Using peers as tutors or guides enhances achievement. Research shows that the use of peers to provide feedback and support improves low achievers' computational abilities. . . . If nothing else, having a

Table 4.3 Mathematics Interventions – Empirical Research	
Intervention	Effect size
Providing stds. with performance data & suggestions	0.57
Weekly instructional suggestions to teachers	0.51
Peer-assisted learning	0.66
Direct or explicit instruction by teacher	0.58
Concrete, weekly, feedback to parents	0.42
Adapted from Baker, Gersten, and Lee, 2002, p62	

partner available to provide feedback is likely to be of great benefit to a low achiever struggling with a problem.

Providing clear, specific feedback to parents of low achievers on their children's successes in mathematics seems to have potential to enhance achievement, although perhaps modestly.

A small body of research suggests that principles of direct or explicit instruction can be useful in teaching mathematical concepts and procedures. This includes the use of strategies derived from cognitive psychology to develop generic problem-solving strategies and more classic direct-instruction approaches (Baker, Gersten, and Lee, 67–68).

Using assessment to improve teaching and student achievement is a principle that comes up often in the educational literature. In fact, a major assessment textbook is titled exactly that, *Test Better, Teach Better* (Popham 2003).

Often, in conducting educational research, only one variable or intervention is studied at a time. In this way, it is possible to find the effect of the intervention or treatment on one or more outcome measures. If several treatments are tried together, it is difficult or impossible to tell which treatment has the effect. This is analogous to a woman having a complete makeover consisting of a new hairstyle, new makeup, and new clothes. After such a makeover, if the woman received a compliment, it would be impossible to know what part of the makeover made the most difference. Common sense would suggest that combining the mentioned treatments into a single intervention aimed at helping struggling mathematics learners would have a cumulative effect but probably not an additive effect.

THE WORK OF LIPING MA

Liping Ma is a highly respected math educator who received her doctorate from Stanford University and as of this writing is a senior scholar at the Carnegie Foundation for the Advancement of Teaching. Ma's research interests are in the study of teachers' content knowledge. Here is an example of the type of deep-content knowledge her research would suggest that teachers need. (The example is taken from an interview with Ma in Herrera 2002, 19)

Many children have trouble with math in third or fourth grade because they do not know all of their addition facts. Table 4.4 shows the 81 addition pairs.

Teachers with a deep knowledge of mathematics would teach the commutative property of arithmetic, i.e., you can add numbers in any order. Children who know this principle do not need to learn, for example, $5 + 6$ because they would know it is the same as $6 + 5$. When the commutative property is applied to the 81 addition pairs, there are 45 remaining pairs, as shown in table 4.5.

According to Ma, most children only have difficulty with the pairs that total more than 10. There are 20 such pairs, as shown in table 4.6.

Table 4.4 81 Addition Pairs								
1+1	1+2	1+3	1+4	1+5	1+6	1+7	1+8	1+9
2+1	2+2	2+3	2+4	2+5	2+6	2+7	2+8	3+9
3+1	3+2	3+3	3+4	3+5	3+6	3+7	3+8	3+9
4+1	4+2	4+3	4+4	4+5	4+6	4+7	4+8	4+9
5+1	5+2	5+3	5+4	5+5	5+6	5+7	5+8	5+9
6+1	6+2	6+3	6+4	6+5	6+6	6+7	6+8	6+9
7+1	7+2	7+3	7+4	7+5	7+6	7+7	7+8	7+9
8+1	8+2	8+3	8+4	8+5	8+6	8+7	8+8	8+9
9+1	9+2	9+3	9+4	9+5	9+6	9+7	9+8	9+9

Adapted from Ma, 2002

Table 4.5 Commutative Property

1+1	1+2	1+3	1+4	1+5	1+6	1+7	1+8	1+9
2+1	**2+2**	2+3	2+4	2+5	2+6	2+7	2+8	3+9
3+1	**3+2**	**3+3**	3+4	3+5	3+6	3+7	3+8	3+9
4+1	**4+2**	**4+3**	**4+4**	4+5	4+6	4+7	4+8	4+9
5+1	**5+2**	**5+3**	**5+4**	**5+5**	5+6	5+7	5+8	5+9
6+1	**6+2**	**6+3**	**6+4**	**6+5**	**6+6**	6+7	6+8	6+9
7+1	**7+2**	**7+3**	**7+4**	**7+5**	**7+6**	**7+7**	7+8	7+9
8+1	**8+2**	**8+3**	**8+4**	**8+5**	**8+6**	**8+7**	**8+8**	8+9
9+1	**9+2**	**9+3**	**9+4**	**9+5**	**9+6**	**9+7**	**9+8**	**9+9**

Adapted from Ma, 2002

Again, teachers with a deep understanding of math could further reduce these 20 pairs down to 11 pairs by teaching students how to add the pairs containing nine. Study the additions below.

$9 + 2 = 11$
$9 + 3 = 12$
$9 + 4 = 13$
$9 + 5 = 14$
$9 + 6 = 15$
$9 + 7 = 16$
$9 + 8 = 17$
$9 + 9 = 18$

Table 4.6 20 Pairs Greater Than 10

1+1	1+2	1+3	1+4	1+5	1+6	1+7	1+8	1+9
2+1	2+2	2+3	2+4	2+5	2+6	2+7	2+8	3+9
3+1	3+2	3+3	3+4	3+5	3+6	3+7	3+8	3+9
4+1	4+2	4+3	4+4	4+5	4+6	4+7	4+8	4+9
5+1	5+2	5+3	5+4	5+5	5+6	5+7	5+8	5+9
6+1	6+2	6+3	6+4	**6+5**	**6+6**	6+7	6+8	6+9
7+1	7+2	7+3	**7+4**	**7+5**	**7+6**	**7+7**	7+8	7+9
8+1	8+2	**8+3**	**8+4**	**8+5**	**8+6**	**8+7**	**8+8**	8+9
9+1	**9+2**	**9+3**	**9+4**	**9+5**	**9+6**	**9+7**	**9+8**	**9+9**

Adapted from Ma, 2002

As you may have noticed, when adding a number to 9, you reduce the number by 1 and increase the 9 by 1. In other words, reduce the one's place by 1 and increase the ten's place by 1. Once children learn this easy way to add the pairs with 9 in them, there are only 11 troublesome pairs left that must be learned by rote memory. Table 4.7 shows the remaining troublesome pairs.

It is interesting to wonder if the teachers in the mathematics-teaching research discussed above, had this deep understanding of mathematics content. Regardless, Liping Ma's research certainly informs practice. For more information, see Ma's book, *Knowing and Teaching Mathematics*. Here are Ma's thoughts on elementary mathematics teachers.

WORDS ON FIRE

Teachers should have confidence in themselves. They are the ones who digest all the knowledge, who listen and change it into a "whole" through their own understanding. I don't know if the word soul is the right word here, but I think teachers are the soul that gives out the light of all the knowledge they hold. I really want them, and us as math educators, to think about that. Otherwise, teachers feel that everybody knows more than they do. Then they lose themselves. I would tell teachers, "Do not forget yourself as a teacher of yourself." (Ma in Herrera 2002, 20)

Table 4.7 12 Troublesome Pairs

1+1	1+2	1+3	1+4	1+5	1+6	1+7	1+8	1+9
2+1	2+2	2+3	2+4	2+5	2+6	2+7	2+8	3+9
3+1	3+2	3+3	3+4	3+5	3+6	3+7	3+8	3+9
4+1	4+2	4+3	4+4	4+5	4+6	4+7	4+8	4+9
5+1	5+2	5+3	5+4	5+5	5+6	5+7	5+8	5+9
6+1	6+2	6+3	6+4	**6+5**	**6+6**	6+7	6+8	6+9
7+1	7+2	7+3	**7+4**	**7+5**	**7+6**	**7+7**	7+8	7+9
8+1	8+2	**8+3**	8+4	**8+5**	**8+6**	**8+7**	**8+8**	8+9
9+1	9+2	9+3	9+4	9+5	9+6	9+7	9+8	9+9

Adapted from Ma, 2002

CONCLUSION

Helping children who are in the lowest 20 percent of their class is a challenge. Given the research in this chapter, several generalizations can be made. First, direct instruction by a qualified teacher or trained adult is the approach of choice. Direct instruction, as the term is used in this chapter, means one teacher working directly with children on the content of the lesson, which must be at an appropriate level of difficulty. Second, working one-on-one with children is a proven intervention that can bring a child up to grade level in as little as one semester's time. Working with children in groups of two or three is also effective, but the same is probably not true for larger groups, which are the norm. Although individualized remedial instruction is expensive in terms of teacher time, it is cost effective when you consider that retaining a child costs about $8,000—the average cost per pupil for a year of school in the United States—which must be paid twice.

Most of the reading interventions discussed above used vast libraries of 2,000–3,000 books and other materials. These libraries had leveled books, which means that the books are, for example, coded as early first grade, middle first grade, and so on. Unfortunately, very few classrooms have such an extensive library.

Most of the interventions with struggling mathematics learners emphasized basic facts and not higher-level skills such as problem solving and geometry. Knowing the basic math facts is seen as a prerequisite to higher-level mathematics learning. From the work of Liping Ma with fourth graders who did not know some of their addition pairs, one has to wonder, how did these children get so far behind, given that addition pairs are usually mastered in first or second grade? From Ma's work, it can be concluded that elementary teachers need a deep understanding of arithmetic, not of algebra and other mathematics they must take in college. This fact has strong implications that apply to teacher-training programs.

Many people mistakenly think that intervention programs like RR are too expensive for a school district to afford. Without such programs, however, many students are mistakenly placed in special-education programs. State funding formulas have a multiplier that funds special-education students at 2 to 2½ times the amount allocated for a regular education student. Thus a special-education student costs the taxpayers $16,000 to $20,000 a year (2 to 2½ times $8,000).

Implementing interventions like those discussed in this chapter has the potential to save large amounts of money.

REFERENCES

Baker, S., R. Gersten, and D.S. Lee. September 2002. A synthesis of empirical research on teaching mathematics to low-achieving students. *Elementary School Journal* 103 (1): 51–73.

Conneautville School District Website. Reading Recovery. Conneautville, PA 16406. [Retrieved from the Internet, April 4, 2006.]

D'Agostino, J.V., and J.A. Murphy. Spring 2004. A meta-analysis of Reading Recovery in United States schools. *Educational Evaluation and Policy Analysis* 26 (1): 23–38.

Herrera, T. (2002). "Do not forget yourself as a teacher of yourself": An interview with Liping Ma. *ENC Focus*. The Eisenhower National Clearinghouse for Mathematics and Science Education 9 (3): 16–20.

Iverson, S., E. Tunmer, and J. Chapman. October 2005. The effects of varying group size on the Reading Recovery approach to preventative early intervention. *Journal of Reading Disabilities* 38 (5): 456–72.

Kroesbergen, E.H., and J.E. Van Luit. March/April 2003. Mathematical interventions for children with special needs: A meta-analysis. *Remedial and Special Education* 24 (2): 97–114.

Ma, L. 1999. *Knowing and teaching elementary mathematics: Teachers' understanding of fundamental mathematics principles in China and the U.S.* Mahway, NJ: Lawrence Erlbaum.

McKenna, M.C., and R.D. Robinson. 2002. *Teaching through text: Reading and writing in the content areas* (3rd ed.). Boston, MA: Allyn & Bacon.

Morris, D., B. Shaw, and J. Penny. 1990. Helping low readers in grades 2 and 3: An after-school volunteer tutoring program. *Elementary School Journal* 91: 133–50.

Neuman, S.B., and D. Celano. 2001. Books aloud: A campaign to "put books in children's hands." *The Reading Teacher* 54 (6): 550.

Popham, J. 2003. *Test better, Teach better: The instructional role of assessment.* Association for Supervision and Curriculum Development.

Reading Recovery. Conneautville School District, Linesville, PA. Retrieved from the Internet on April 4, 2006, http://connwww.iu5.org

Santa, C.M. 1998. *Early Steps: Learning from a reader.* Kalispell, MT: Scott.

Santa, C.M., and T. Hoien. Jan/Feb/Mar 1999. An assessment of Early Steps: A program for early intervention of reading problems. *Reading Research Quarterly* 34 (1): 54–79.

Therrien, W.J. July/Aug 2004. Fluency and comprehension gains as a result of repeated reading: A meta-analysis. *Remedial and Special Education* 25 (4): 252–61.

U.S. DOE, Office of Research. 1992. *Education consumer guide: Reading Recovery.* Office of Research, p. 1.

Worthy, J., R.S. Patterson, S. Prater, and M. Turner. Winter 2002. More than just reading: The human factor in reaching resistant readers. *Reading Research and Instruction* 41 (2): 177–202.

5

Size Matters: Class Size and School Size

Unfortunately, many people confuse—sometimes purposefully—class size and pupil-teacher ratio. Class size is simply the number of children in a single classroom with a single teacher. Pupil-teacher ratio is the number of children in a school divided by the number of certified teachers. A school's pupil-teacher ratio is always much lower than its class size because there are a lot of teachers in a school who are not classroom teachers. Typically, a school of 800–1,000 students has four resource teachers (physical education, art, music, and computer), one or more librarians, several special-education resource teachers, and a remedial-reading teacher. Often the school's principal and assistant principal are also certified teachers, so they get included in a school's pupil-teacher ratio. A school district's pupil-teacher ratio is an even more distorted statistic since many administrators at all levels are also certified teachers. Only about 50–60 percent of a school district's employees are classroom teachers. Twenty years ago, this figure was 70 percent.

COTEACHING

States that have passed class-size reduction (CSR) legislation—for example, Tennessee, California, and Florida—have generally tried to reduce class size in kindergarten through third grade (K–3) to

17 or 18 to 1. Because it is difficult for districts to quickly add the necessary classrooms, some have resorted to what has become known as "coteaching." Coteaching involves placing 34 children and two teachers in a single classroom. Since most K–3 classrooms are designed for 24–28 children, this obviously makes for a crowded room. And since coteaching has only recently been tried, there is little research evidence on its effectiveness. One thing is certain: the research conducted on CSR without coteaching cannot be generalized to classrooms with coteaching.

RESTRICTED RANGE ISSUE

If classrooms with 30 children are compared to classrooms with 27 children, very little, if any, differences would be found in achievement or teaching method. The reason is simple: the range from 30 to 27 is "restricted," as researchers term it. Consider an analogy of buying a new car. If you had $20,000 to spend on a new car and managed to add $1,000 to your budget, it is unlikely that you could buy a significantly better or fancier car. On the other hand, if you added $10,000 to your $20,000, you could probably buy a much nicer car.

Obviously, the optimum class size is one-to-one. That is a primary reason why educational interventions like Reading Recovery (discussed in chapter 4) work so well. At the other extreme, a class size of 100-to-1 would certainly be undesirable. The question then becomes, what is the optimum class size in the range of 1 to 100?

OLSON'S LANDMARK RESEARCH

In the early seventies, Martin Olson, of Teachers College–Columbia reported on a large-scale research project involving thousands of classrooms across the United States. He studied the relationship between class size and a composite classroom measure called "Indicators of Quality." This highly reliable and valid instrument was designed to assess classroom processes on four dimensions: individualization, interpersonal regard, group activity, and creativity.

In 11 metropolitan areas, 18,528 school rooms, in 112 largely urban school districts were visited by trained observers who used the Indicators of Quality instrument to give each classroom a numeric score on each of the instrument's dimensions. Composite Indicators of Quality scores were then compared to classroom characteristics such as class size and number of adults in the room.

Interestingly, Olson discovered that the classroom quality took a substantial upswing as class size was reduced across certain boundaries. This relationship is similar to the cost of stamps at the post office. A letter or package costs the same price to mail until its weight crosses a certain level. See table 5.1. In the elementary school, the largest jumps in quality occurred when class size was reduced to 25, to 15, and to 5 students. At the secondary level, the largest jumps in quality occurred when class size was reduced to below 15 and to below 10.

Another way to look at Olson's findings is that if you have 30 students in an elementary school classroom and you reduce the number

Table 5.1 Quality Indicators by Class Size

Class Size	Scores Elementary	Scores Secondary
Under 5	10.64	8.31
5-10	8.34	**8.45**
11-15	**8.34**	6.25
16-20	7.26	4.77
21-25	6.45	4.25
26-30	4.73	3.93
31-35	4.66	3.51
36-40	3.17	4.41
41-50	4.38	3.65
50+	2.22	3.22

Total Observations = 9,961

Adapted from Olson, September 1971, p64

of students to 29, or 28, or 27, or 26, it will not have a large effect. If, however, you reduce the number of students to 25 or less, you can expect a sizeable improvement. The same can be said about the other boundaries—you must get to or below them to make much difference. Incidentally, Olson's study is one of the few studies that examines secondary-school class size. Here is Olson's conclusion.

WORDS ON FIRE

With little question, it would be well for school systems to consider altering their class size ratios if close to and on the wrong side of a critical breakpoint, such as 26–1 ratio in the elementary school. However, to expend school funds to lower just any existing ratio one or two students seems entirely unjustified in view of this evidence. (Olson, 65)

Olson also examined the relationship between type of classroom activity observed and quality. In both elementary and secondary schools, small-group work and laboratory work received the highest scores. In addition, Olson examined the relationship between the number of adults in the classroom and quality. According to Olson, "In no case at either grade level did greater numbers of adults in the classroom affect scores as significantly as one might imagine. In fact, most recorded scores were near to lower than the one adult situation" (Olson, 65). This last finding may shed some light on the practice of coteaching discussed earlier. Additionally, the Tennessee CSR study discussed later helps to confirm this last finding.

THE TENNESSEE STAR PROJECT

One of the largest, most well-designed, experimental studies of class size was the Tennessee STAR Project (Student/Teacher Achievement Ratio), which was conducted from the mid- to late eighties. In the mideighties, the Tennessee Legislature funded a four-year study that started with 6,325 kindergarten students in 80 schools in inner city, urban, suburban, and rural schools. In the first phase of the study, kindergarten students and teachers were randomly assigned to one of three experimental conditions: a small class size (17 or fewer students), a normal class size (22–25 students), and an augmented class (22–25 students) with a teacher and a full-time, uncertified, teacher aide. (Ran-

Table 5.2 STAR Results – Small Classes Months of Grade Equivalent Advantage in Reading Spring of Third Grade	
No. Yrs. in Small Classes	Months Advantage
4	7.1
3	5.2
2	3.3
1	1.5
Adapted from Finn et al, 2001, See Reference Note 1.	

domization helps eliminate selection and assignment bias in a study.) Schools were given funding to hire the extra teachers needed, but they were not given money to cover other costs. Students remained in the three types of classrooms from kindergarten through third grade. Efforts were made to keep the curriculum and materials used the same across the three types of classrooms. (See reference note 1)

The second phase of the class-size study, called the Lasting Benefits study, was a quantitative comparison that studied the children as they progressed from kindergarten to third grade. In each year of the study, all students were given the Stanford Achievement Test and the Tennessee Basic Skills test in the spring. Table 5.1 shows the results for reading of project STAR students who were in small classes for from one to four years.

Two things are noteworthy about the Project STAR results. First, the effect of small classes is cumulative over time. The longer a child is in a small classroom, the greater the benefit. Second, students who were in small classes from kindergarten through third grade were nearly a year ahead of other students in reading—7.1 out of 9 months in a school year. Results were similar, but slightly smaller, for mathematics.

Wondering about the long-term effects of small classes, the Tennessee legislature funded a follow-up study of project STAR students who had been in small classes for one or more years. By the time they reached eighth grade, project STAR students were 4.1 months ahead in reading, 3.4 months ahead in mathematics, 4.3 months ahead in science, and 4.8 months ahead in social science. Remember, these results are for students who spend one or more years in small classes and not for students who were in small classes for all four years.

The follow-up study found a host of other benefits that STAR students enjoyed, including higher grade averages, fewer dropouts, higher graduation rates, and greater participation in advanced-level high school courses. Across all phases of the STAR project, the benefits of small classes were particularly pronounced for low-income students and African American students. On some outcome measures, this group benefited twice as much as other students.

CLASS-SIZE REDUCTION:
THE WISCONSIN SAGE PROJECT

Under the direction of noted Arizona State University researcher Alex Molner, the Wisconsin Student Achievement Guarantee in Education (SAGE) project began during the 1996–1997 school year. Funded by the Wisconsin legislature, the SAGE project and study focused its efforts on school districts with at least 50 percent of their students living below the poverty level. The SAGE project began in 30 schools in 21 school districts in kindergarten and first grade in 1996.

Unlike project STAR, some of the schools participating in project SAGE tried arrangements such as assigning two teachers to a large classroom (termed "coteaching" earlier), fitting temporary walls within large classrooms, and employing "floating teachers" who moved from classroom to classroom. The SAGE schools were compared to schools from the same district with similar family incomes, racial makeup, and prior achievement-test results. The SAGE classrooms achieved results quite similar to the STAR classrooms. As in the STAR project, relatively larger gains were found for African American students. SAGE results indicated that classrooms with two teachers (coteaching) and classrooms with "floating teachers" did not show significant gains.

As a result of the SAGE project, the Wisconsin legislature has made small class size in the early grades available to all schools serving low-income students. This large scale, statewide, implementation of class-size reduction nearly eliminates matched classrooms that can serve as comparison classrooms.

CLASS-SIZE REDUCTION: CALIFORNIA

In 1996, then-governor of California, Pete Wilson, announced a new policy that would provide $600 per student (later raised to $800) to all elementary schools that would agree to reduce class size to not more than 20 students per classroom. As an educational intervention, the California initiative had many factors working against its success. The SAGE project provided $2,000 per participating student compared to California's $600–800. Also, the California initiative reduced class sizes to fewer than 20 students, which was a smaller reduction than in previous class-size-reduction efforts. At the time of the California initiative, schools in California were severely overcrowded due to large and steady population growth. This placed extra space burdens on already overcrowded schools. Even with these problems, the California initiative showed modest gains for participating classrooms. Opponents of class-size-reduction efforts and class-size-reduction legislation often point to the failure of the California initiative, but given the design and the constraints under which it operated, such results might be expected.

CLASS-SIZE REDUCTION: LONG-TERM EFFECTS

Way too many educational interventions show an immediate effect on the performance of students, but oftentimes these benefits seem to diminish, if not vanish, quickly. Class-size reduction in grades K–3 is a different story. In 2001, Jerome Finn and colleagues published a follow-up study designed to answer the question, "Do the benefits of small classes in grades K–3 have lasting effects that can be measured in grades, 4, 6, and 8?" Here is the researchers' answer to this question.

WORDS ON FIRE

In addition to immediate impact, attending small classes also had long-term benefits. In general, students who attended small classes in K–3 performed significantly better academically on all subjects in grades 4, 6, and 8 than their peers who attended full-size classes. . . . Four years in a small class put students nearly a whole school year ahead of their counterparts who had attended larger classes. (Finn 2002, 174)

Five years after returning to large classrooms in the fourth grades, students were still benefiting from being in small classrooms in the primary grades. Few, if any, educational interventions show anywhere near as enduring an effect.

CLASS-SIZE REDUCTION: THE ACHIEVEMENT GAP

In 2003, Phil Smith, Alex Molner, and John Zahorik took a fresh look at the SAGE data to help answer several questions including, "Does attending small classes in grades K–3 have an effect on the achievement gap between African American and White students?" Here is the researchers' conclusion.

WORDS ON FIRE

By the end of first grade, their [African American] achievement scores were significantly higher than those of African Americans students in larger classes. They also narrowed the achievement gap that had separated them from their white classmates at the start of 1st grade. In the 2nd and 3rd grade, the academic performance of African-American students in small classes kept pace with that of their white peers.

African-American students seem to profit more from the SAGE experience than white students. When compared with non-SAGE students, the SAGE program narrows the achievement gap between African American and white in the 1st grade and prevents it from widening in 2nd and 3rd grade. In the larger comparison classrooms, the achievement gap between African American and white students widens every year. (Smith et al. 2003, 73)

After separate and thorough reviews of the class-size-reduction literature, two prominent education scientists offered the following conclusions:

WORDS ON FIRE

Class-size reduction is sound educational policy. It has been shown to be effective time and again, and no serious challenge has been made to the research findings that support these conclusions. Educators have long known this.

Research has now documented the advantages of small classes, especially in elementary grades and especially for students who attend small classes for two,

three, or four consecutive years. *The effects are especially pronounced for minority students and those attending schools in large urban districts. As a result
the achievement gap [between white and minority students] is reduced both in
the years while students attend small classes and later on when they consider
applying to college.* (Finn 2002, 13)

WORDS ON FIRE

*Reducing the size of classes for students in the early grades often requires ad-
ditional funds, although sizeable educational benefits result when this step is
taken. Students from all walks of life reap long-lasting advantages, but students
from educationally disadvantaged groups benefit particularly. Indeed, if we
judge by available evidence, no other educational reform has yet been studied
that would provide such striking benefits, so debates about reducing class size
are basically disputes about values. If Americans are truly committed to providing quality public education and a level playing field for children regardless of
background, once they learn about the advantages of small classes in the early
grades, they will presumably find the funds needed to reduce class size.* (Biddle
and Berliner 2002, 25)

SCHOOL SIZE

Starting in the sixties, with the publication of James Conant's book *The
Comprehensive High School*, school districts started building larger and
larger high schools with more and more students and with a wide variety of curricular offerings. At the time, it was believed that high schools
needed to be large in order to support expensive programs such as advanced placement, distributive education, auto mechanics, wood shop,
agriculture classes, and vocational-education classes of all kinds. The
comprehensive-high-school movement persisted until nearly the end
of the century. Even today, it is not uncommon to find high schools
with 2,000 to 3,000 students. Large elementary schools with over 1,000
students are also common. In the late nineties, reformers began think-
ing that large schools are impersonal, uncaring places where students
easily get lost. Compared to studying classrooms, studying schools is
substantially more difficult. Schools are larger and more complicated
places than classrooms, and studying them requires much more sophisticated techniques. Often the research design and the statistical
techniques used in such studies are difficult to explain—especially to

the layperson. For this reason, some of the research reviewed below will have less detail than research discussed earlier in the book.

Researchers can study main effects or interaction effects. An example of a main effect is a study of the relationship between single variables such as school size and achievement. An example of an interaction effect is a study of the relationship between two or more variables such as the relationship between district size, school size, and achievement. For example, researchers might use categories such as large district, large school; large district, small school; small district, large school; and small district, small school. Another example of an interaction effect is the relationship between school size and poverty on achievement. Often, interaction effects are much more substantial than single main effects.

Socioeconomic status (SES) is a term for family income. In many research studies, the percentage of students who receive free or reduced price lunch in a school is used as a measure of the number of low-SES children in a school. This is often the only data that is universally available. Obviously, a school with less than 25 percent of the children on free or reduced price lunch is a much different school than one with over 75 percent of the children on free or reduced price lunch.

TEXAS HIGH SCHOOL STUDY, 2001

In 2001, the researchers reported on an investigation of the effect of school size as it interacted with SES on achievement in 1,001 Texas high schools. Here are the researchers' conclusions.

This line of research has, with unusual consistency, found an interesting interaction effect between socioeconomic status (SES) and school size in the production of achievement: as school size increases, school performance (aggregate achievement at the school level) decreases for economically disadvantaged students. In short, as schools get larger, those with poor children as students perform increasingly less well when achievement is the outcome measure. School size imposes increasing "achievement costs" in schools serving impoverished communities.

An interesting interaction effect which has been found in replications across seven very different states is that as school size increases, the "achievement test score costs" associated with the proportion of economically disadvantaged students enrolled in a school also increase. In short, as schools get larger, average achievement among schools enrolling larger proportions of low socioeconomic-status students suffers. (Bickel et al. 2001, 2)

As with seven previous analyses, we have found that as school size increases, achievement-test-score costs associated with having economically disadvantaged students in schools also increase. This finding has now proven robust across seven states and across at least four different regression model specifications. This degree of consistency is rare indeed in educational research.

This study once again corroborates the manner in which SES regulates the relationship of school size to school performance. The findings have proven to be unusually robust, which makes them difficult to dismiss. (Bickel et al. 2001, 25)

WASHINGTON STATE STUDY, FOURTH AND SEVENTH GRADES

In 2002, the Washington School Research Center (WSRC), an independent research and data analysis center at Seattle Pacific University, conducted a study to see if they could replicate the results of the Bickel and colleagues's study, discussed above, using Washington State data. This study, however, also investigated the effect of district size on achievement. The study title clearly shows its intent: *The Influence of District Size, School Size, and Socioeconomic Status on Student Achievement in Washington.*

Data for this study were provided by the Washington State superintendent of public instruction, and the data consisted of all fourth and seventh grade scores on the Washington Assessment of Student Learning (WASL) for reading and mathematics. Student scores were aggregated to the school level.

Jeffrey Fouts, executive director of the research center, offered this conclusion to the study.

WORDS ON FIRE

The WSRC researchers conclude: *"We found that large district size is detrimental to achievement in Washington 4th and 7th grades in that it strengthens the negative relationship between school poverty and achievement."* Further they state, *"The negative relationship between school poverty and achievement is stronger in larger districts, and small schools appear to have the greatest equity effects." In other words, when school poverty is high, children perform better in small districts, and the effect of school level poverty on achievement is smallest when both district and school are small.* (Abbott, Joireman, and Stroh 2002, 5–6)

The achievement gap between black and white students and between low- and high-SES children is a major concern of educators and policymakers. The WSRC study provides evidence that the achievement gap between poor and affluent children is the least pronounced in small schools and small districts. In other words, a small school reduces the effects of poverty on children.

It would be unwise, however, to assume that simply creating small schools would guarantee success for low-SES students. School size is a necessary, but insufficient factor to guarantee their success. The next study sheds some additional light on what makes a small school effective.

NEW YORK CITY HIGH SCHOOL STUDY, 2002

In late 2002, researchers from Stanford and Teachers College–Columbia reported the results of a seven-year effort in New York. This study describes the outcomes associated with the replacement of two large, comprehensive, neighborhood, New York City high schools with 11 smaller schools. Each of the large high schools served about 3,000 students, the smaller replacement schools about 450 students each. In the year the study began, 1992, the two large high schools had graduation rates of 36.9 percent and 26.9 percent. This project of the New York City schools was dubbed the Coalition Campus Schools Project (CCSP). The National Center for Restructuring Education, Schools, and Teaching collected data throughout the project.

Expenditure or cost per pupil is a common educational statistic— see chapter 3. Graduation rates like those for the two schools reported above have prompted educational researchers to believe that a better statistic might be *cost per graduate*. Thus, a school with a graduation rate of 50 percent would have twice the cost per graduate as a school with a graduation rate of 100 percent. Perhaps in the future, such a statistic will become more common.

In contrast to many of the research studies discussed in this chapter, this study did not just study smaller high schools. Instead, the intervention included teaching a pared-down, core college-prep curriculum and a school organization consisting of small interdisciplinary teams of teachers with 40 to 80 students. These teams of teachers often worked with the same group of students for two or more years. Plus, all class periods were 90 minutes in length. Thus, the study investigated the effects of creating *innovative* small schools, not just small schools.

This study was termed "mixed mode research." Translated, this means that the study used both qualitative and quantitative techniques. On the qualitative side, researchers conducted hundreds of interviews with school-board members, principals, teachers, parents, and students. In addition, dozens of classroom observations were conducted over the course of the study.

Quantitative aspects of the study included collecting numeric data on important indicators such as attendance, student achievement, graduation rates, and so on. Table 5.3 shows a comparison between the average NYC school and the CCSP schools for the 1998–1999 school year. Notice that even though the CCSP schools served more disadvantaged students, their annual dropout rate was about half that of NYC schools. Remember that annual dropout rate is yearly and that over the four high school years it accumulates. And, as discussed in chapter 2, the national annual dropout rate is approximately 5 percent.

Table 5.4 shows several other indicators of CCSP schools' success during the 1995–1996 school year. Notice the improvement in attendance, discipline, and reading gains. In the table, LEP stands for "limited English proficiency," another term for "English as a second language" students.

Table 5.3 Demographic & Dropout Data NYC vs. CCSP		
Characteristic	NYC avg.	CCSP avg.
% resource rm participants	4.4	9.5
% English language learners	15.6	23.3
% Free lunch	44.2	72.2
Annual drop out rate	6.7	3.4
Adapted from Darling-Hammond, Ancess & Ort. Fall 2002, p651		

Table 5.4 Std. Outcomes NYC vs CCSP Schools

Indicator	NYC	CCSP
Avg. daily attendance	85	86.2
Discipline incident rate	3.5	1.2
Suspension rate	5.6	3.2
% stds. making reading gains	43.6	56.9
% LEP stds. making reading gaines	65.4	91.2

Adapted from Darling-Hammond, Ancess, & Ort, Fall 2002, p647

Here are some of the qualitative aspects of the research. According to the researchers, "several factors were consistently identified by respondents—and confirmed by our observations and document review—as important in the schools' success. These included (a) small size; (b) structures that allowed for personalization and strong relationships; (c) a carefully constructed curriculum aimed at specific proficiencies; (d) teachers' pedagogical approaches, especially their explicit teaching of academic skills and their ability to adopt instruction to students' needs; (e) a school-wide performance assessment system; (f) the creation of flexible supports to ensure student learning; (g) strong teachers supported by collaboration in planning and problem solving" (Darling-Hammond et al., 653).

Two techniques used in qualitative research are to collect data through interviews and on-site observations. These data are reported in transcript form and direct quotes, which get voluminous. Often, qualitative research is reported in book-length volumes. In order to save space, only a small sample of this data is reported here.

INTERVIEW COMMENTS

There is less violence here compared to bigger schools. Everyone knows one another. Bigger schools are louder and crazier. No one will bother you here.—student

We and the teachers are very close.—student

You are just not going to fall through the cracks here. You are an important individual.—student

School should not be mass production. It needs to be loving and close. That is what kids need. You need love to learn.—student

I was bad all the way back from elementary and junior high school. I would have got lost in the system. I would not have made it. I would have dropped out. I needed someone to be there to show me they care about me for me to be motivated.—student

Small size means I can do a literature seminar with the bottom 20 percent of kids in the city. Kids who didn't read are reading books like *Jane Eyre* to write their essays. We work with them during lunch. We find out who can't read, type, etc. These are the kids who would sit in the back of the room, be in the bathroom, and would deliberately get lost.—teacher

This school will get the worst student to do the work.—student

I can use in-depth approaches and assign college-level research projects. For two months, each morning, we teach students' research skills and essay skills so they can do a minimum-20-page research paper in history. . . . They choose the topic. We develop their topic together.—teacher

I spent more time reading the books. If I didn't understand, teachers here would explain the material. They gave me other books. I took the midterm and did O.K.—student

Teachers share what they are doing in a formal way in team meetings. They plan together and share what they have done. There is a whole school sharing and there are summer institutes where we have more time to reflect. There is more coherence than in bigger schools where teachers work alone.—teacher

From Darling-Hammond, Ancess, and Ort 2002, 655–63.

WORDS ON FIRE

Breaking down anonymity is important in all schools, especially in poor urban systems where kids do not have a support system. Big schools have a hard time doing this. Small schools create a culture that kids buy into and

*that their parents feel is responsive and [where] faculty feel they can make
a difference. But small is not enough. Schools need professional development
and commitment of staff and commitment of parents and kids that they have
to do things differently. We need to create schools where teachers and kids
can have relationships. Relationships have to be used to get good academics.*
(Margaret Harrington, Chief Executive Officer for K–12 instruction,
DOE, in Darling-Hammond et al., 668)

In 2006, Aimee Howley and Craig Howley, two researchers who have
spent many years investigating small schools, summarized this body
of research as follows:

WORDS ON FIRE

*Although many of the claims currently made for smaller schools under the press
of the changed conventional wisdom are difficult to warrant empirically, several are comparatively well established: (1) impoverished children have higher
achievement in smaller schools, (2) the link between poverty and achievement
is weaker in smaller schools as compared to larger schools, (3) dropout rates
are lower in smaller schools, (4) participation rates in school activities are
much higher in smaller schools, and (5) smaller schools can offer appropriate
curriculum.* (Howley and Howley 2006, 4)

REMAINING ISSUES

Missing from the research literature on small schools is any consensus
about how small is small. The number most frequently mentioned for
elementary schools is 200–450 students. For high schools the most
frequently mentioned number is 250–650 students.

Another remaining issue is, how old are the school buildings in
the United States? This is an important question because the research
reviewed above would indicate that when we replace old school
buildings with new ones, we should keep a close eye on the size of the
new schools. The age of U.S. school buildings is an almost impossible
statistic to generate because of renovations and additions made to
existing school buildings. Reading data from the National Center for
Education Statistics, it would seem that about 35 percent of all school
buildings in the United States are more than 50 years old. Other
experts put the number closer to 50 percent. Regardless, it is safe to

conclude that we have a large number of aging schools that may soon need to be replaced or substantially renovated.

A third issue is the effectiveness of the school within a school (SWS) method of breaking up large schools. A "pure" SWS school has a distinct faculty, its own budget and principal, and it is totally autonomous from the larger school. It is rare to find such autonomous SWS schools. Many SWS efforts have failed because the faculty members don't seem to like being segregated from the larger school environment.

CONCLUSION

Taken collectively, the research on class size and school size gives us insights into how we might reform schools to better serve students. Logically, combining the positive effects of smaller classes in smaller schools might have a strong interaction effect. Research supporting this logic, however, is not extant. Policymakers at every level would do well to consider size as a significant variable in any discussion of school effectiveness.

REFERENCES

1. Several-dozen, well-respected researchers have been involved in and/or written about the class-size-reduction research. Jerome Finn, University of New York–Buffalo, was a lead researcher for the Tennessee STAR project. Alex Molner of Arizona State University was a lead researcher on Wisconsin SAGE project. These primary references are listed below.

Finn, J.D., S.B. Gerber, C.M. Gerber, and J. Boyd-Zaharias. 2001. The enduring effects of small classes. *Teachers College Record* 103 (1): 114–83.

Molner, A., P. Smith, J. Zahorik, A. Palmer, A. Halbach, and K. Ehrle. 2000. Evaluating the SAGE program: A pilot program in targeted pupil-teacher reduction in Wisconsin, *Educational Evaluation and Policy Analysis* 21 (2): 165–77.

Abbott, M., J. Joireman, and H. Stroh. 2002. The Influence of district size, school size and socioeconomic status on student achievement in Washington: A replication study. Washington school research paper.

American Architectural Foundation and Knowledgeworks Foundation. 2006. *National Summit on School Design: A Resource for Educators and Designers.* Retrieved March 1, 2007 from http:archfoundation.org.

Bickel, R., C. Howley, T. Williams, and C. Glascock. October 8, 2001. High School Size, Achievement Equity, and Cost: Robust Interaction Effects and Tentative Results. *Education Policy Analysis Archives* 9 (40). Retrieved February 6, 2007 from http://epaa.asu.edu/epaa/v9n40.html.

Biddle, B.J., and D.C. Berliner. Winter 2002. What research says about small classes and their effects. Education Policy Reports Project, EPSL-Educational Policy Studies Laboratory, Arizona State University. Available from http://edpolicyreports.org.

Conant, J.B. 1967. *The Comprehensive High School*. New York: McGraw-Hill.

Darling-Hammond, L., J. Ancess, and S.W. Ort. 2002. Reinventing high school: Outcomes of the Coalition Campus Schools Project. *American Educational Research Journal* 39 (3): 639–73.

Finn, J.D. 2002. Class-size reduction in grades K–3. In A. Molner (ed). School reform proposals: The research evidence. Educational Policy Research Institute, Arizona State University, EPSL-0201-101-EPRU. Available at http://www.asu.edu/educ/epsl/reports/epru.

Howley, A., and C.B. Howley. Small schools and the pressure to consolidate. *Education Policy Analysis Archieves* 14 (10). Retrieved January 30, 2007 from http://epaa.asu.edu/epaa/v14n10/

Olson, M. September 1971. Research notes: Ways to achieve quality in school classrooms: Some definitive answers. *Phi Delta Kappan*: 63–65.

Smith, P., A. Molner, and J. Zahorik. September 2003. Class-size reduction: A fresh look at the data. *Educational Leadership* 61 (1): 72–74.

6

Assessment and High-Stakes Testing

Although various writers would describe the birth of the high-stakes testing movement differently, two factors clearly contributed to it. First, in 1993, the U.S. Department of Education issued a report entitled, *Prospects: The Congressionally Mandated Study of Educational Growth and Opportunity*. Here is one of the report's major findings: "Prospects data depict stark differences in academic achievement between students in high-poverty schools and those in low-poverty schools. Regardless of the grade level, there are large differences in reading and math scores between students in low- and high-poverty schools, especially in higher-order cognitive skills. On average, students in low-poverty schools score from 50 to 75 percent higher in reading and math than students in high-poverty schools" (Puma et. al. 1993, xxx) (ERIC ED 361466). Clearly there was an achievement gap, and maybe one cause was TESA.

TESA

TESA is an educational acronym that stands for "Teacher Expectations Equals Student Achievement," sometimes displayed as TE=SA. Simply stated, the principle means that if you don't expect students to do well, they probably won't. Or visa versa, if you expect students to do well, they probably will. At their best, teachers would have high expectations of every student. Teachers' expectations, however, may be influenced by track or group placement, classroom conduct, physical appearance, race, family income, speech characteristics, and type of school—for example, inner city versus urban (Good and Brophy 1991, 121). "Teacher expectation effects in classrooms are just special cases of the most general principle that any expectation can become self-fulfilling. Sometimes, our expectations about people cause us to treat them in ways that make them respond just as expected" (Good and Brophy 2003, 70).

Many politicians and policymakers began to believe that the reason why students in high-poverty schools did so poorly was because teachers and others had such low expectations of them. The solution seemed obvious: the nation needed standards that every student must master. As Vogler wrote, in a rather tongue-in-cheek way,

> The blueprint to achieve educational accountability is seemingly quite simple. First design statewide curriculum for each content area—a "framework" that includes standards and benchmarks for each grade level. Then, to make sure teachers follow and teach this curriculum, mandate statewide tests to assess students' knowledge of the curriculum. Oh, one more thing, attach high stakes for all those involved (e.g., administrators, teachers, and students) to the results of these tests to make certain the curriculum is taught and learned. (Vogler 2005, 9)

It sounds simple, but the research in this chapter shows otherwise.

DEFINITION OF "HIGH STAKES"

High-stakes tests are those that have consequences attached to their results. In 2002, Audrey Amrein and David Berliner of Arizona State University found the following consequences attached to the results of mandated testing in various states:

- The state has the authority to close a school, revoke a school's accreditation, take the school over, or reconstitute low-scoring schools.
- Monetary rewards are given to high-performing or improving schools.
- Monetary rewards can be used for teacher bonuses.
- The state has the authority to replace principals or teachers due to low test scores.
- Grade-to-grade promotion is contingent upon a promotion exam.

- The state permits students in failing schools to enroll elsewhere.
- Monetary rewards or scholarships for college tuition are given to high-performing students (Amrein and Berliner, December 2002, 7).

Incidentally, the first consequence was the most frequently used, and Delaware was the only state with all of the above consequences attached to its test results.

At any given time, it is nearly impossible to determine the number of states with high-stakes tests since different states have different consequences and the consequences may change over time as state legislatures and departments of education change their regulations. In the study mentioned, Amrein and Berliner classified 27 states as the "highest stakes" test states. Today this number is larger due to pressure from the federal government through legislation called the No Child Left Behind Act (NCLB). This act has a provision that specifies that every student in America must make Adequate Yearly Progress (AYP). Essentially this provision states that every year, each of the 46 million school students should make a year's worth of progress in school. The problem with the idea of AYP is that all students do not learn at the same rate. Regardless, the NCLB Act has increased the pressure on states to create and use high-stakes tests, and now nearly all states do so.

A SHORT PRIMER ON EDUCATIONAL ASSESSMENT

The discipline of educational assessment is highly conceptual with a language all its own—sometimes flippantly labeled "educanese." Since the research on assessment is reported using these terms and concepts, knowledge of a few essential ideas and terms is helpful to the reader.

Assessment is a general term for measurement and evaluation. Obviously, many different measurements should be taken before a student is evaluated or graded. And measurements should be both valid and reliable. A valid test measures what it should measure. That is, the content of the test is well aligned with what was taught. For example, if a biology teacher spent half a semester on plant and animal cells, then half of the semester test should be on the cell. Furthermore, the questions on the semester test should use the same kind of language in describing the cell as the teacher used in class.

A reliable test is one that is accurate and consistent. Many factors contribute to reliability including an appropriate number of items— the Goldilocks principle, correct answer key, appropriate writing for the grade level, accurate scoring, and tabulating of results. A consistent test gives roughly the same results every time it is used. Obviously, a test must be reliable to be valid. This can be likened to putting gas in your car. If you get the correct amount of gas (validity), the pump has to be accurate (reliability).

There are two major types of evaluation: criterion-referenced and norm-referenced. Evaluation is concerned with the "compared to what" issue. In criterion-referenced evaluation, a student is compared to a set of content standards, a set of objectives, or a list of skills. Criterion-referenced evaluation often implies keeping track of how many things a student has learned or can do. In contrast, norm-referenced evaluation compares an individual student to a group of students. Terms like "above average, average, and below average" are the result of comparing a student to a mathematical mean score.

It follows then that norm-referenced tests are designed to compare individual students to what is called a "national norm group" of children. Since it would be impossible for a test manufacturer to measure the four million students at any grade level, the test maker carefully selects a group of several thousand students that is assumed to be a representative sample of the whole population. It is important to remember that when a student takes a nationally norm-referenced test, that student is compared to the norm group of children and not to students in his class, school, district, or state. States that design their own tests can decide on what, or to whom, they want to compare their students. Therein lies the problem in using any state-level test results to judge the quality of state schools.

AMREIN AND BERLINER'S 2002 STUDY OF THE STATES

For this study, the researchers had two objectives. "The first objective of this study is to assess whether academic achievement has improved since the introduction of high-stakes testing policies in [grades K–8] in the 27 states with the highest stakes written into their grades K–8 testing policies. If academic achievement did not change after stakes were attached to a state test or if achievement decreased, the effectiveness of the high-stakes policy as a means of improving student performance must be called into question" (p. 2).

"The second objective in this study is to assess whether academic achievement has improved after the introduction of high school graduation exams. In the 18 states with high school graduation exams, students must pass these exams before they are graduated. If academic achievement did not change after the implementation of a high school graduation exam, the effectiveness of the high school graduation exam policy as a means of improving student performance is called into question" (p. 2).

For several reasons, the researchers did *not* use the results of each state's tests as a measure of achievement. First, states regularly change their tests, making year-to-year and state-to-state comparisons difficult. Second, state-mandated test results often improve over time, but the improvement is probably related to a training effect. A training effect would occur if students were trained in test-taking skills, taught a narrow set of skills to a high level of proficiency, made to memorize answers to questions they would likely encounter, and taught only the subjects measured on the tests, such as mathematics and English, at the expense of other subjects.

Because of these issues, the researchers used state NAEP (National Assessment of Educational Progress) test results for grades K–8 achievement. For high school achievement, the researchers used three measures: the SAT (Scholastic Aptitude Test), the ACT (American College Test), and AP (Advanced Placement) scores. These tests assess the same domains of knowledge as the state-level tests, with the possible exception that these tests may be broader in coverage. That is, they place a greater emphasis on problem solving and on subjects such as science and the humanities, and on topics in social studies such as economics.

Here are the researchers conclusions about high-stakes tests in grades K–8. "No consistent effects of state-mandated high-stakes testing across states were noted. Scores seemed to go up or down in a random pattern, after high-stakes tests are introduced, indicating no consistent state effects as a function of high-stakes testing policy" (Amrein and Berliner, December 2002, 57). The researchers had this to say about high school graduation exams:

WORDS ON FIRE

The data presented in this study also suggest, however, that after the implementation of high school graduation exams, academic achievement apparently decreases. After high school graduation exams were implemented, achievement as indicated by ACT, SAT, and AP scores declined. Indeed, on balance, these analyses suggest that high-stakes tests and high school graduation exams may inhibit the academic achievement of students, not foster their academic growth. (Amrein and Berliner, December 2002, 58)

MARCHANT AND PAULSON'S REPLICATION AND EXTENSION OF THE AMREIN AND BERLINER STUDY, 2005

In 2005, Gregory Marchant and Sharon Paulson of Ball State University reported the results of a study that replicated and extended the Amrein and Berliner study discussed earlier. The researchers investigated the relationship between high-school-graduation exams to SAT scores and graduation rates. Marchant and Paulson found consistently negative relationships between state exams and educational outcomes. Students in states with required high-school-graduation exams scored lower on the SAT test than students in other states. Three years had elapsed since the Amrein and Berliner study, but the results were similar. Whereas Amrein and Berliner did a state-by-state analysis, Marchant and Paulson aggregated the state data. Thus, two different ways of looking at the same issue yielded the same result. In educational research, replication of results such as this is highly persuasive.

For this research, the following data were used: Amrein and Berliner's classification of states (18 states with graduation exams and 33 without, including D.C.), enrollment by grade level and

Table 6.1 State Graduation Requirements		
	No Graduation Exam	Graduation Exam Required
Graduation Rate	72%	64%
Average SAT Scores	1,078	1,044
Adapted from Marchant & Paulson, 2005, p6		

graduation rates, state percent minority students, family income (percent free or reduced lunch), percent special-education students, and SAT test results. Examining the aggregated data, the researchers found support for prior research that found that states with high-school-graduation exams "tended to have more minorities and more students eligible for free or reduced [price] lunch programs" (Marchant and Paulson 2005, 5).

"States with a graduation exam requirement averaged a 64 percent graduation rate, 8 percentage points lower than the 72 percent for the states without the requirement" (Marchant and Paulson 2005, 6). Eight percentage points might not seem like much, but if there are 4 million students at any grade level, then 320,000 students fail to graduate each year in the United States because of this one cause. Furthermore, "The use of high school graduation exams had a significant negative impact on individual SAT scores" (p. 7).

Here are the researchers comments.

WORDS ON FIRE

Students struggling to succeed in high school might very well find one more hurdle is one hurdle too many. The fact that these adolescents were more likely to be minorities and from lower SES backgrounds was particularly disturbing. The students that have worked perhaps harder than most to overcome obstacles, it seems unconscionable to establish a policy that places a potentially insurmountable barrier between them and a diploma. Colleges report their pools of applicants, especially minority applicants, are being reduced by high school graduation exam requirements (Schmidt 2000). Even if the high school graduation exams were not a barrier to a diploma, it may still be a barrier to higher education.

. . . in the absence of substantial benefits from the practice [the use of required graduation exams], and the growing evidence of negative consequences, in addition to the expense in time and money, any efforts to increase the use of graduation exams seems ill advised. Justification for the continuation of the practice needs to be clearly established beyond past assumptions. Too much is at stake for too many to base educational policy on assumptions, good intentions, or political interests. (Marchant and Paulson 2005, 12)

MARCHANT, PAULSON, AND SHUNK, 2006

In 2006, Gregory Marchant, Sharon Paulson, and Adam Shunk, of Ball State University, reported the results of a comprehensive study of high-stakes testing. Unlike most other studies, these researchers controlled for family demographic factors—specifically, family income, highest levels of education that parents completed, ethnicity, and percent of students in the state who were excluded from the test due to disability or to limited English language proficiency. These variables are known to vary substantially from state to state. All state NAEP data in all four subjects—English, math, science, and social studies—were considered from 1992 to 2002. The researchers used single-year data and data spanning four-year time periods. The primary research questions were, "Do changes in achievement scores differ between states with and without high-stakes testing?; do the demographics of the testing samples predict their achievement?; and with demographic differences controlled, do indicators of high-stakes testing policies predict the achievement of the testing samples?" (Marchant et al. 2006, 5).

Controlling for the demographic factors mentioned above equalizes any differences in these important attributes that exist from state to state. Many educational researchers believe that any study that does not control for these kinds of variables yields questionable results. Here are the results of this comprehensive study.

"Results revealed that across all testing samples, there were no differences between those [states] with high-stakes testing and those without high-stakes testing on either *reading* scale scores or percentage of students reaching Basic on the reading achievement portion of the NAEP." (p. 8)

> "Analysis showed that writing proficiency did not differ between states with and without high-stakes testing." (p. 13)
>
> " . . . high-stakes testing indicators did not add to the prediction of any of the *science* achievement measures." (p. 20) In other words, science achievement was unrelated to high-stakes testing.
>
> "Results revealed that *math* achievement did not differ between states with and without high-stakes testing." (p. 16)

Here are the researchers overall conclusion.

WORDS ON FIRE

In light of the expense and unintended negative consequences being indicated by the research, the bottom line question concerning high-stakes testing must

*be, is high-stakes testing worth it as a general approach to educational reform?
If this type of testing did not take much time or cost much money, the lack of
consistent evidence supporting achievement would not be important. However,
the Government Accountability Office estimates that states will spend between
$1.9 billion and $5.3 billion in the next six years.* (Olson 2004, 23–24)

TIME DEVOTED TO TESTING

Very little has been written about the amount of time that is taken away
from instruction that is then devoted to local, state, and federal testing.
Here is an example from Duval County, Florida, the fifteenth-largest
school district in the nation. Responding to the federal mandate that
every student make AYP, the district has decided to test elementary
school students three times a year, in September, December, and April.
Unfortunately, one cannot give young children—for example, first
graders—a group-administered, paper-and-pencil test. Instead, one
must test each student individually. Using the test that the district
has chosen takes about 20 minutes per child to administer. Testing
three students a day takes the teacher about two weeks. Given that
this testing is to be done three times a year, the total reading time
devoted to testing and not to instruction is six weeks per school year.
There are 36 weeks in a school year, so this testing takes one-sixth of
a year. That is a lot of time taken away from instruction.

NATIONAL BOARD ON EDUCATIONAL
TESTING AND PUBLIC POLICY

An excellent source of objective information on testing is the National Board on Educational Testing and Public Policy (NBETPP),
which is located in the Lynch School of Education at Boston College.
The National Board is supported by grants from a number of philan-
thropic organizations such as the Ford Foundation and the Atlantic
Philanthropies. For more information, and for the latest research
and news, visit their Website at http://www.bc.edu/nbetpp.

In 2003, the board released three major studies on high-stakes testing. The first study, by Marguerite Clark and others (January 2003),
was titled *Perceived Effects of State-Mandated Testing Programs on
Teaching and Learning: Findings from Interviews with Educators in Low-,*

Medium-, and High-Stakes States. The researchers interviewed 120 edu-cators in each of three states: Kansas, a low-stakes state; Michigan, a medium-stakes state; and Massachusetts, a high-stakes state.

Educators in states along the continuum from Kansas to Michigan to Massachusetts had somewhat different perceptions of the positive and negative impact of state testing. These differences across the state continuum, however, were not radically different, and educators in all three states often had similar views. "Between half and three-quarters of the educators in each state expressed neutral to positive opinions about state standards, mentioning that they encouraged a greater cur-ricular consistency across schools as well as an increased emphasis on problem solving and writing. Kansas and Massachusetts interviewees were the most positive in this regard. At the same time, a sizable mi-nority (between one-fifth and one-third of interviewees in each state expressed concerns about the negative effects of the standards on classroom practice—among them, that they could lead to develop-mentally inappropriate material [content not appropriate for age of student] and pace, curriculum narrowing, and decreased flexibility. Massachusetts (a high-stakes state) teachers were the most likely to mention this concern (Clark et al. 2003, 4).

Here are several other findings from this study.

In all three states, elementary educators reported the greatest impact of the state standards on classroom practice. (p. 5)

Educators in the rural districts appeared to find it the hardest to align their local curriculum with the state standards. The most frequently men-tioned concerns included a lack of curriculum materials, few professional development opportunities, and the potential loss of local identity as a result of aligning with the more context-free state standards. (p. 5)

In all three states, educators were deeply concerned about the social studies content standards. Their worries included the following: too much content to cover, developmentally inappropriate material, and an emphasis on facts rather than concepts.

In all three states, only one out of ten interviewees felt that the state test had no impact on how they taught. (p. 6)

Furthermore, only about one-fourth of the educators thought that the state tests had a positive influence on student learning. Here are the researchers' conclusions.

WORDS ON FIRE

*There is a need to make the teaching and learning process an integral part
of the standards-based reform and to recognize that testing should be in the
service, rather than in control, of this process. This refocusing increases the
chance of deep, rather than superficial, changes in student knowledge.* (Clarke
et al., 12)

PEDULLA AND OTHERS NATIONAL
SURVEY OF TEACHERS, 2003

In 2003, Joseph Pedulla and others at the NBETPP reported the results
of a national survey of teachers that was conducted to find the perceptions of teachers about state-mandated testing programs. The researchers sent a long, well-designed survey to 12,000 teachers. The number
of surveys returned was 4,195, for a return rate of 35 percent. Researchers prefer higher return rates because one has to wonder whether the
surveys that weren't returned would change the study results. Still, it is
difficult to ignore the thoughts of over 4,000 teachers.

The study found that overall, elementary and middle-school teachers felt more pressure from state-mandated testing programs than secondary-school teachers. (This is consistent with the first NBETPP study
discussed above.) And as one might expect, teachers in higher-stakes
test states and those in tested grades felt more pressure than teachers
in lower-stakes test states and grades. In fact, "Between 3 in 10 and
4 in 10 teachers in higher-stakes states reported that teachers at their
school wanted to transfer out of tested grades" (Pedulla et al. 2003,
2). This rather unfortunate finding has far-reaching implications.
Many teachers'-union school-board contracts require that teachers
spend about three years in one position before they can transfer to
a different school or grade. The result is that teachers in tested grade
levels often have less experience since the more experienced teachers
can transfer out. There is anecdotal evidence that in some schools, all
the teachers at a tested grade level have less than three years of experience. This is unfortunate since tested grade levels are where students
need the most help.

Another finding was that "Three-quarters of all teachers, regardless of stakes or grade level, found that the benefits of the testing
programs were not worth the time and money involved." About an
equal percentage of teachers felt that the media coverage was unfair

and that it did not accurately portray the quality of education at their school (p. 4).

Not surprisingly, teachers reported that they spent more time covering tested subjects and less time teaching other subjects. They also reported using more direct instructional techniques such as whole-group instruction and individual seat work, and using problems similar to those on the tests (p. 4). This finding is consistent with other results reported in this chapter.

The researchers also found evidence of what is termed, "educational triage." Triage is the sorting of students into three groups: students who can easily do well on the test, those who have little chance of doing well, and students who can easily be helped to do well on the test. Triage means to concentrate instruction on the third group of students—the group that will benefit most from instruction. Here is how the researchers explained this finding: "Teachers in high-stakes states were more likely to report that they focused test preparation on students who were on the border either of passing or of moving to the next performance level" (p. 5). Unfortunately, the researchers did not report the number or percentage of teachers who said they focused their attention in this manner. Given a typical elementary school, if as few as 30 students perform better on the test than they did in the past, it can substantially improve the overall school results.

In summary, this research reported finding that state-mandated testing programs often have unintended consequences. Policymakers who implemented the state-mandated testing programs apparently did not envision all that might happen as a result of their policy decisions.

An obvious question about high-stakes tests is, how do high-stakes tests affect teachers who teach the types of courses assessed by them? The next two studies help shed light on this question.

VOGLER'S STUDY OF HIGH SCHOOL SOCIAL STUDIES TEACHERS

In 2005, Kenneth Vogler, of the University of Northern Iowa, reported the results of a study that surveyed 107 Mississippi high school U.S. history teachers to find out how a high-school-graduation exam that covered the content of their courses might influence their instructional practices. Of the 107 teachers surveyed, 89 teachers, or 83.2 percent reported spending class time preparing their students to take the test. A substantial number of teachers reported spending over two months of class time preparing for the exam.

In the survey, 90 percent of the respondents reported that the graduation test affected the instructional practices they used. Teachers who spent the most class time preparing for the exam reported using more teacher-centered teaching techniques as compared to more student-centered techniques. Examples of teacher-centered techniques are lectures, lectures with discussion, textbook assignments, drill and practice worksheets, sample quizzes, and so on. Examples of student-centered techniques are inquiry activities, current events, individual use of technology, cooperative learning, and simulations.

The comments of a Mississippi U.S. American history teacher to the survey are presented here.

WORDS ON FIRE

I use the entire academic year preparing my students for the United States history subject area exam. My choice of instructional delivery and materials is completely dependent on preparation for the test. I do not use current events, long-term projects, or creative group/corporate work because this is not tested and the delivery format is not used. All my tests reflect the testing format of the subject area tests—multiple choice and open-ended questions. This delivery and curriculum format is [sic] not used in my other classes (United State Government and Economics). *I agree with the principle of student/teacher/ administrator accountability, but by making the goal of my United States history course the ability to pass the state test, I'm afraid that all meaningfulness and relevancy to history is being lost on my students. As a result, they have a better factual base but a worse conceptual understanding of the subject and what it is good for.* (Vogler 2005, 2)

In 2006, the researcher did nearly the same study with Tennessee high school biology teachers. In the Tennessee study, 74.3 percent of the teachers reported spending over two months preparing their students for the high-school-graduation exam. As in the Mississippi study, teachers used predominantly teacher-centered instructional techniques such as worksheets, supplementary materials, textbook assignments, and lectures. Twelve of the fourteen least used instructional practices were student-centered. (Vogler 2006, 7)

You might ask why using predominantly teacher-centered techniques would be considered a negative outcome of the use of high-school-graduation exams. The answer is simply that high-stakes tests reduce teacher flexibility. Good teachers use a wide variety of different techniques including indirect techniques. Poor teachers tend to use one or a few techniques.

CHILDREN'S PERCEPTIONS OF HIGH-STAKES TESTING, TRIPLETT AND BARKSDALE

Cheri Foster Triplett and Mary Alice Barksdale of Virginia Polytechnic Institute did a fascinating study that involved having 225 third through sixth graders in five elementary schools in two states give their impressions of high-stakes testing the day after they finished taking the state test. The students were asked to "Draw a picture about [their] recent testing experience." After they finished their pictures, the students were asked to "Tell me about your picture" (Triplett and Barksdale 2005, 241). Using sophisticated qualitative-research techniques, the researchers derived eleven categories in which to classify the students' drawings and writings. The three most common classifications were "accouterments of testing, isolation, and emotion." The first two classifications were present in over half the drawings and writing. Emotion was present in 32 percent of the drawings and writings (p. 243).

In order to analyze drawings and writings classified in the emotions category, the researchers divided the student work into words and facial expressions. The following were frequently used words: "nervous, mad, sad, frustrated, hate, confused, bored, tired, sweating, and sleepy. Related terms that were frequently used to describe the tests were 'too long,' 'hard,' 'easy,' 'dumb,' and 'crazy.' 'Nervous' was the emotion most frequently discussed" (p. 244).

Anger was another common emotion in the children's work. Here is an example.

> I felt mad and frustrated about HST and was feeling so mad. I felt like I wanted to do well. But I did not, and I felt like I was in a crazy house, and I got even more mad when it got harder. Then we took a break. Then I felt a little good. But the second half I felt like I wanted to cry, and I started feeling like I wanted to spit on the test. But then we finished. (p. 245)

According to the researchers, "In analyzing the drawings, it was very clear that they had intentionally drawn unhappy and angry expressions. Smiles were nearly nonexistent. There were many frowns, mouths formed in waves and straight lines, mouths with tongues sticking out, sharp-toothed mouths, and faces with tears. Additionally, there was much use of question marks in their drawings and 'Help' was written in speech bubbles above their heads" (p. 245).

The researchers concluded, "These findings convincingly support previous research reporting that elementary children experience high levels of nervousness and anxiety about high-stakes testing" (p. 255). Furthermore, from this and prior research, it is obvious that children are well aware of the consequences of high-stakes, such as grade retention, that are attached to state-mandated tests. Perhaps teachers and parents could do more to lessen children's test anxiety. It is likely that heightened test anxiety negatively influence test results.

ERRORS IN STANDARDIZED TESTS

Using funding from the Ford Foundation, the NBETPP released a paper titled, "Errors in Standardized Tests: A Systematic Problem" (NBETPP 2003, May). This paper was a culmination of several years work collecting and documenting published reports of testing errors that were and were not detected by testing companies. The researchers reported 52 errors not detected by testing contractors, 26 errors detected by testing contractors, and 18 errors in rank ordering schools or students.

Here are a few abbreviated examples of the kinds of errors reported by the researchers. In 1996, the Philadelphia district superintendent of schools announced that Harcourt Educational Measurement had admitted to scoring errors on the Stanford Achievement Test (SAT9). The error caused two schools to be classified as needing remedial help even though their test scores had actually improved. The schools were removed from the list of schools needing "drastic action," action that included staff transfers. Harcourt Brace was fined $192,000 for this incident (NBTEPP 2003, 35).

In 2001, the Arizona Department of Education held back AIMS writing test scores after observing large incongruities between 2000 and 2001 scores. An investigation revealed calculation errors in the third and fifth graders' scores. Subsequently, NCS/Pearson, the test maker, employed Arizona teachers to re-grade the tests (p. 47).

In 2002, the staff at Vanguard Middle School, in the Houston Independent School District, discovered a clerical error in which students were erroneously designated as "dropouts," which caused teachers to miss out on $800 per person in bonus money. Subsequently, the school petitioned the district for the bonus money (p. 52). The researchers concluded the following:

WORDS ON FIRE

Human error can be, and often is, present in all phases of the testing process. Error can creep into the development of items [test questions]. It can be made in the setting of a passing score. It can occur in the establishment of norming groups, and is sometimes found in the scoring of questions.

The decisions that underlie the formation of cut scores and passing scores are largely subjective. Glass (1997) pointed out that the idea of objectively setting cut scores that accurately differentiate between students who know and students who don't know is largely a fantasy—there is no clear distinction and no mathematical or logical support for such an idea in the realm of educational testing. (NBETPP 2003, 28)

Gene Glass's 1997 paper, referenced earlier, was a thorough, theoretical, statistical, and commonsense discussion of setting absolute performance levels—also called "criterion levels" or "cut scores." The paper has stood the test of time and is a must-read for those interested in knowing more about the problems associated with the arbitrary setting of "cut scores." Here is Glass's summary.

I am confident that the only sensible interpretation of data from assessment programs will be based solely on whether the rate of performance goes up or down. Interpretations and decisions based on absolute levels of performance on exercises will be largely meaningless, since these absolute levels vary unaccountably with exercise content and difficulty, since judges will disagree widely on the question of what consequences ought to ensue from the same absolute levels of performance, and since there is no way to relate absolute levels of performance to success on the job at higher levels of schooling or life. Setting performance standards [cut scores] on tests and exercises by known methods is a waste of time.

In education, one can recognize improvement or decay, but one cannot make cogent, absolute judgments of good or bad. (Glass 1977, 35)

The National Board study on errors in testing documented an incident that clearly illustrates how dire the consequences can be when

ment of Education (DOE) gave one school the grade of C. The
school's principal notified the DOE that they had omitted a high-
scoring student's score from the school totals. The DOE responded
and recalculated the school's grade, this time including the high-
scoring student's score. This recalculation raised the overall school
score from 49.5 percent to 50.0 percent of the students passing the
state test. This raised the school's grade from a C to an A (NBETPP
2003, 52).

THE COST OF TESTING

It is nearly impossible to accurately estimate how much money is
spent annually testing the nation's students. One reason is that the
large corporations that produce and sell tests are quite secretive.
Another reason is that information on the amount of money states
spend either on purchasing or developing, administering, and scoring
the tests they use or make is often not available. One thing is certain,
though: testing is a big business. According to Marguerite Clarke and
others at the National Board, approximately 17 million students are
tested annually and some are tested several times (Clarke et al. 2001,
2). This works out to be about a third of the nation's students. In most
school districts, students are tested every two to three years.

The testing market is dominated by a few large corporations including ACT, Inc., McGraw-Hill, Educational Testing Service (ETS), NCS
Pearson, Riverside Publishing/Houghton-Mifflin, Scantron, and Harcourt Educational Measurement.

Here is an example of the cost of testing a single class of 25 students
using the Stanford Achievement Test, Ninth Edition, Complete Battery (SAT9). The SAT9 is not a single test. Rather, it is a test battery
covering most school subjects. The figures below were obtained from
the Harcourt Website in the summer of 2007.

* Machine scrabble test booklets	$217.00
* Answer documents	$ 61.75
* Directions for administering	$ 20.80
* Scoring key	$ 48.10
* Class record	$ 9.10
Total	$350.75

Dividing the above total by 25 students yields a per-pupil cost of $14.03. This figure does not include computer time, test-scoring machine, labor to perform the scoring, time and cost to print individual student and class records, and the labor required to distribute the results. Factor in these kinds of expenses, and the per-pupil-cost could easily reach $30. If there are 1,000 students in a school, the total cost comes out to $30,000.

Things are never as simple as they seem, as Lawrence Baines and Gregory Stanley pointed out in the *Educational Forum*.

WORDS ON FIRE

One unanticipated problem with high-stakes testing is that administrative costs have been not one-time debits, but continuous expenses. To keep up with the paperwork, state governments have created bureaucracies within bureaucracies— Offices of Educational Accountability, Offices of Test Administration and Reporting, Offices of Standards and Measurement—while simultaneously reducing their staff, including teachers to stay within their budget.

The annual cost of high-stakes testing rivals the gross national product of some small countries, somewhere between $20 and $50 billion, or about 5.5 to 14 percent of every dollar spent for public Schools. (Baines and Stanley 2004, 8)

Assessment is obviously important, but assessment for the purpose of high-stakes decision-making is a separate issue. No one would argue that we do not need to assess students to find out if our instructional efforts are producing results. Since testing costs a great deal of money, however, we should perhaps use testing for its intended purpose. And we should assess judiciously.

THE PROBLEM OF USING A SINGLE TEST

"Measure twice, cut once," is an old woodworker adage that also applies to testing school students. You wouldn't want to miss-cut an expensive piece of lumber. Likewise, using a single test to make an important decision about a student is dangerous. Simply put, more measurements yield more accurate results than a single measurement. Yet most states and many school districts give what are often called, "single-shot high-stakes tests." All too often, a single test is used to decide whether a child should be promoted or retained or even whether a student will graduate from high school.

Many professional associations and teachers' unions oppose the "inappropriate use of tests to make high-stakes decisions including the American Evaluation Association, the American Educational Research Association, the National Council For Teachers of English, the National Council for Teachers of Mathematics, the International Reading Association, the College and University Faculty Assembly, the National Council for the Social Studies, and the National Education Association" (American Evaluation Association 2007, 5).

Here is the position statement of the American Evaluation Association (AEA): "High-stakes testing leads to underserving or mis-serving all students, especially the most needy and vulnerable, thereby violating the principle of 'do no harm.' The AEA opposes the use of tests as the sole or primary criterion for making decisions with serious negative consequences for students, educators, and schools. The AEA supports systems of measurement and accountability that help education" (AEA 2007).

The AEA summarized what they consider "Violations of AEA Guiding Principles and Other Professional Standards" by making the following observations. "Many high-stakes testing programs

- channel educational offerings to satisfy monolithic, narrow, test-defined state standards rather than address the differential needs of students in local schools;
- narrow the curriculum to tested subjects, usually reading, writing, mathematics, and marginalize nontested subjects, which often include the fine arts, physical education, social studies, and science;
- consume a disproportionate amount of student and teacher time that takes away from other valued school goals and activities, e.g., spending as much as 30 percent of the school year preparing specifically for tests;
- assume that all children, including English-language learners and special-education students learn in the same way at the same rate and that they can demonstrate their achievements on standardized tests;
- focus attention on particular students such as those scoring just below the cutoff score and ignoring those who score well above

and below the cutoff score." [This is called "educational triage," author.] (AEA 2007, 3)

The American Educational Research Association's position on high-stakes testing is that ". . . every high-stakes achievement testing program in education should meet all of the following conditions: [list is abbreviated]

- Protection against high-stakes decisions based on a single test.
- Adequate resources and opportunity to learn.
- Validation of each separate intended use.
- Alignment between the test and the curriculum.
- Validity of passing scores and achievement levels. [Not arbitrarily choosing a passing score.]
- Opportunities for meaningful remediation for examinees who fail high-stakes tests.
- Appropriate attention to language differences among examinees.
- Appropriate attention to students with disabilities.
- Careful adherence to explicit rules for determining which students are to be tested.
- Sufficient reliability for each intended use.
- We urge, 'Ongoing evaluation of intended and unintended effects of high-stakes tests'" (American Educational Research Association 2007, 2–3).

CONCLUSION

High-stakes testing programs are in place in the hope that they will improve achievement, but the evidence shows that they do not. There is also evidence that high-stakes testing programs have a more-deleterious effect on minority students, special-education students, and English-as-a-second-language students. Given that massive amounts of money are spent on such programs annually, one has to wonder if this money might be better used to help the third of our students who never graduate from high school.

REFERENCES

American Educational Research Association. 2007. AERA position statement on high-stakes testing in pre-K–12 education. pp. 2–3. Retrieved 07/02/2007 from http://aera.net/policyandprograms/id=378&terms=high+stakesandsearchtype=2&fragment=false.

American Evaluation Association (AEA). 2007. Position statement on high stakes testing in pre-K–12 education, p. 1. Retrieved from http://www.eval.org/hst3/htm on 7/02/2007.

Amrein, A.L., and D.C. Berliner. December 2002. The impact of high-stakes tests on student academic performance: An analysis of NAEP results in states with high-stakes tests and ACT, SAT, and AP test results in states with high school graduation exams. Tempe, AZ: *Educational Policy Studies Unit*. Retrieved from http://epsl.asu.edu/epru/documents/EPSL-0211-126-EPRU.pdf.

Baines, L.A., and G.K. Stanley. Fall 2004. The high-stakes hustle: Public schools and the new billion dollar accountability. *The Education Forum* 69 (1): 8–15.

Clarke, M., C.H. Madaus, C. Horn, and M. Ramous. April 2001. The Marketplace for Educational Testing. Boston College: *National Board on Educational Testing and Public Policy Statements* 2 (3). Retrieved on August 15, 2007 from http://www.bc.edu/nbetpp.

Clarke, M., A. Shore, L. Rhoades, L. Abrams, J. Miao, and J. Li. January 2003. Perceived effects of state-mandated testing programs on teaching and learning: Findings from interviews with educators in low-, medium-, and high-stakes states. Boston College: *National Board on Educational Testing and Public Policy*. Retrieved on August 15, 2007 from http://www.bc.edu/nbetpp.

Glass, G. 1977. "Standards and Criteria." Occcasional Paper Series, 10. Retrieved from http://www.wmich.edu/evalctr/pubsops/ops10.html.

Good, T.L., and J.E. Brophy. 1991. *Looking in Classrooms, Fifth Edition*. New York: HarperCollins.

Good, T.L., and J.E. Brophy. 2003. *Looking in Classrooms, Ninth Edition*. New York: Allyn and Bacon.

Marchant, G.J., and S.E. Paulson. January 2005. The relationship of high school graduation exams to graduation rates and SAT scores. Tempe, AZ, *Educational Policy Analysis Arrchives* 13 (6). Retrieved from http://epaa.asu.edu/epaa/v13n6.

Marchant, G.J., S.E. Paulson, and A. Shunk. 2006. Relationship between high-stakes testing policies and student achievement after controlling for demographic factors in the aggregated data. *Educational Policy Analysis Archive* 14 (30): 1–34. Retrieved August 2007 from http://epaa.asu.rfu/epaa/12n30.

Olson, L. December 1, 2004. NCLB law bestows bounty on test industry. *Education Week* 24 (14): 1, 18–19.

Pedulla, J.J., L.M. Abrams, G.F. Madaus, M.K. Russell, M.A. Ramos, and J. Miao. March 2003. Perceived effects of state-mandated testing programs on teaching and learning: Findings from a national survey of teachers. Boston College: National Board on Educational Testing and Public Policy.

Puma, M.J., C.C. Jones, D. Rock, and R. Fernendaz. July 1993. Prospects: The congressionally mandated study of educational growth and opportunity: The Interim Report. U.S. Department of Education, Washington, D.C.

Schmidt, P. January 21, 2000. Colleges prepare for the fallout from state testing policies. *The Chronicle of Higher Education*, A 26–28.

Triplett, C.F., and M.A. Barksdale. Summer 2005. Third through sixth graders' perceptions of high-stakes testing. *Journal of Literacy Research* 37 (2): 237–58.

Vogler, K.E. 2005. Impact of a high school graduation examination on social studies teachers' instructional practices. *Journal of Social Studies Research* 29 (2): 19–34.

Vogler, K.E. 2006. Impact of a high school graduation examination on Tennessee science teachers' instructional practices. *American Secondary Education* 35 (1): 33–58.

7

Discussion, Implications, and Recommendations

"This book is about science." That was this book's first sentence. It is important to remember that the science in this book will evolve over time. Some of the research discussed in the first six chapters will be supported and refined, and some may even be refuted. Still, some of the science is persuasive. For example, it is hard to imagine that the 100+ studies showing the negative effects of grade retention will be discredited.

In research, it is customary for researchers to state a study's findings without offering their interpretations, explanations, or recommendations. In research reports, this section is usually labeled "Findings." After this section, the researcher is then free to offer interpretations and explanations. In research reports, this section is often labeled, "Discussion." This book has more-or-less followed this tradition by saving a discussion of the research covered until this, the final chapter. The discussion that follows will comment on the research, show that it is interconnected, and allow me to offer suggestions.

THE UNINFORMED

Unfortunately, the vast majority of educators—at all levels—know very little of the research. (If this statement were false, I wouldn't have written this book.) We have an immense body of knowledge that can help kids, but most educators and policymakers don't even know that it exists. That is too bad, and it needs to change. Education professors and school principals need to read, disseminate, and discuss the research—they have a professional obligation to do so. The obvious question is, why do so many educators know so little about the research literature? Is it the nature of the education profession? Is belief so omnipotent that it always trumps science? Is it that researchers don't take the time or go to the trouble of explaining their research to the layperson? Is it that the time demands of teaching and running schools is so pressing that educators have no energy left to stay informed? All of the above are answers, but the time demands of teaching and of running schools simply leave no time or energy left for educators to stay informed.

Here is an example that supports the last contention. In the fall of 2007, a teachers' union in a large city sent the following postcard to thousands of teachers.

This madness has to stop!
It's about respect and dignity!!!
ATTENTION: ALL union members

The union will be addressing the School Board at the next meeting. We are encouraging all teachers to attend if you are experiencing any of the following:

- Do you feel you have <u>no</u> freedom in designing your instruction?
- Is "downtown" micromanaging your curriculum?
- Are you overwhelmed with paperwork and testing?
- Do you feel that there aren't enough hours in the day?
- Do you feel that your work is not valued?

Please try to attend the School Board meeting.

THOUGHTS ON TEACHING

Teaching is too big a job! Anyone who has spent a lot of time in schools working with teachers will readily tell you that we cannot add one more thing to their work days. If we are to expect teachers to know the education science, we will have to find time for them to first read it.

Although it varies from one school district to another, here is a typical day in the life of a first-grade teacher in a large urban district: Arrive at school at 7:30 a.m. to prepare for the day. Every few days, have an 8:00 conference with a parent. Students arrive at 8:30. At 11:30, start the 30-minute lunch period by walking students to the cafeteria. Return to the classroom office at 11:40. Pick up students from the cafeteria at 12:00. If weather permits, take children to the playground area for exercise, and stay there to supervise them. Children are dismissed at 3:00, and the last one leaves by 3:15. Two days a week, students go to a resource room (art, music, physical education, computer, or media center) for 20–30 minutes. On some days, have a conference with parents at 4:00. Leave school at about 4:45. It is not the starting or ending time of the typical day that is the problem. Rather it is the more-than-six hours in constant contact with the children with only a 20-minute lunch break. Teaching is an exhausting job. If it is important for teachers to know the education science—and I believe it is—then we have to provide time for them to learn it during the day.

As a profession, education needs to somehow put a higher priority on understanding education science. It is somewhat ironic that in nearly every education course, students are required to buy textbooks that cover every topic under the sun but that rarely summarize research on the topics covered. Maybe professors should start requiring students to purchase journals that report on recent educational research. Reading educational research needs to be an integral part of every education course starting with Introduction to Education.

I would also call on every professional organization to make a greater effort to synthesize and summarize educational research for their members and to distribute it widely and inexpensively both to members and nonmembers. In addition, school administrators need to chisel out time every week for the faculty to study and discuss the research.

CHILD REARING AND THE SCHOOL EFFECT

I once was in an argument with a very bright educational sociologist who won the argument hands-down by arguing that the "school effect" had a much weaker effect on children than societal factors. The sociologist was correct, as the research summarized in chapter 3 shows. Academically and emotionally, children start school radically different, and some of them start school far behind their peers. Unfortunately, the children who start behind stay behind as they grow and move through the grades. The radical differences in children rarely decrease over time since schools treat all students more or less equally. We must find ways to level the playing field so that all children come to school ready to learn. This is the biggest challenge facing our society. Perhaps we can teach people to be better parents and to better prepare their young children for school.

Ironically, most schools require students to pass high school algebra to graduate. No school I know of requires a "How to be a Parent" course. Decades ago, many schools required all students—even boys—to take home economics, which often covered child rearing. I once heard a professor in the College of Arts and Sciences say, "Don't confuse a liberal education with a useful education." Maybe a high school education should be more useful. Maybe people can learn to be better parents. It is worth a try.

Another reason why children start schools unequally is family income. It isn't the money that makes a difference—although it affects nutrition and health care. It is the advantages that affluent children have. Examples of the advantages that higher income children have include summer vacations, books and encyclopedias, computers with Internet access, YMCA [Young Men's Christian Association] membership, and twice-a-year visits to the pediatrician. Obviously, poor parents have a tough time providing these kinds of things for their children. This is especially discouraging since childhood poverty rates are increasing in this country, not decreasing.

Although the term was not used earlier, "transgenerational transfer" contributes to the radical differences in children. There is a strong relationship between parents' highest level of educational attainment (high school dropout, high school graduate, and college graduate) and readiness for school. This causes a viscous cycle of poorly educated parents, poorly educated children, and so on. During the early childhood years, parents' knowledge and skills are critical.

Educators are not responsible for the ills of society, and we should not believe, even for a minute, that schools can fix everything that is wrong in a country. The school effect is not powerful enough. If we truly want to have more successful students, we need to fix a lot of things that have nothing to do with schools. Alas, politics gets involved in this area, and politics is not the subject of this book.

HOPEFUL RESEARCH

Even though the picture painted by the research on "Radical Differences" is discouraging, hopeful research findings were also reported. Examples include the "Babies and Books" research and the research on book gifting, or flooding day care centers with books. And programs like "Reading Recovery," discussed in chapter 4, also give hope. More on things we can do to help kids who are behind after a discussion of flunking kids.

GRADE RETENTION

The "Radical Differences" discussed in chapter 3 help explain why so many students are retained at each grade level. William Glasser, the noted author and psychologist, was fond of saying, "If it doesn't work, quit doing it." We should apply this truism and quit retaining children; it obviously does not work. The misguided practice harms children. Furthermore, anyone who has read chapter 3 and then continues to support grade retention has a closed mind—or they will likely make the argument that retention is better than social promotion.

Social promotion is a derogatory label that supporters of retention use when students are promoted who supporters believe should be retained. Given the immense number of children who are retained each year, it would be impossible to demonstrate that social promotion even exists today. Rather, social promotion is, by-and-large, an imaginary practice. In reality, there is a false dichotomy between retention and promotion. In between these two extremes is the simple idea of remediation. Most schools have a three-month summer vacation so we have a built-in window of opportunity between grade levels. And most teachers don't work during the summer, so we have a waiting workforce of potential tutors.

In my graduate classes, I often ask teachers if they would be willing to work one-on-one with a floundering student for $30 an hour over the summer. They almost universally agree that they would like such a job. Then I ask my students who are elementary teachers if they would be willing to guarantee that their tutee would be reading on grade level by the end of 100 hours. Again, the teachers answer yes. If we could do this, it would obviously cost $3,000 per student, but this is a lot cheaper than the $8,000 it would cost for the student to repeat a grade level. Not long ago, I asked an associate superintendent of a large school system what he thought of the idea. He said, "It makes too much sense. The problem is," he said, "the state will pay me for the student to repeat a grade, but not for summer programs or remedial instruction like this."

We need to quickly give the potential retainee the extra help needed to perform on grade level! Legislators and state education officials should be lobbied to make catch-up programs for faltering students a reality. Not only is this sound policy, but as a friend of mine is fond of saying, "We have the technology," which roughly translates into "We know how to do that." The programs discussed in chapter 4, such as Reading Recovery, have shown a high success rate. We know how to bring 85 percent or more of the lowest quartile students up to grade level in 20 weeks for a cost of about $3,000.

Students who perform below grade level in math are a different story. In doing the research on safety nets and remedial programs in chapter 4, I found a great deal less research that would tell us how to help students who are failing in math. More research should be directed into programs designed to help students who are struggling in math. Case in point, the U.S. Congress mandated a massive effort to study reading instruction called the "National Reading Panel." Although the procedures used by this study team were dubious and their results unreliable, it does demonstrate that the nation, as a whole, cares more about reading programs than math programs. We need a national effort so that we can know as much about how children learn math as how they learn to read.

CLASS-SIZE REDUCTION (CSR)

Reducing class size to 17 students per classroom in grades K–3 is sound educational policy. CSR is the best way we know of to ensure that students will be successful during their entire educational career. As the old saying goes, however, "It's simple, but not easy." The problem is, CSR must be implemented properly in order to be beneficial—often it is not. Placing 34 students and 2 teachers in a single classroom—called "coteaching"—is definitely not CSR. Coteaching often becomes team teaching, which can slip into turn teaching, where the two teachers take turns teaching all 34 students. In the research literature, there is no evidence that coteaching works as well as CSR or that it works at all.

CSR creates a gigantic facilities problem since it requires a large increase in the number of classrooms needed. Logically, there are at least three ways to provide more classrooms: (1) increase the facilities budget and construct more classrooms, (2) make hard choices and shift the district budget around in order to make classroom space the highest priority, and (3) add portable classrooms on every school campus. The third option costs somewhere between what the first and second options cost. In the literature, there is anecdotal evidence that some school districts have creatively solved the facilities problem with minimal increases in their budgets.

CSR may or may not create a teacher shortage. Logically, fewer students per teacher equates to more teachers. It then follows that we need to train and certify more teachers. This logic doesn't work out to be exactly true. In the United States, only 30–50 percent of all the people certified to teach are doing so. In reality then, we don't have a shortage of teachers; we have underemployment of teachers. And when these unemployed teachers are asked why they are not teaching, one of the first reasons given is "working conditions." Reducing class size to 17 students per teacher certainly makes for better working conditions and might persuade some of the unemployed teachers to return to the classroom.

Another way to provide the teachers needed to implement CSR is to require school districts to reduce the percentage of nonteaching employees from the present level of 50 percent to 40 percent, or even to 30 percent. Furthermore, if we redirected that portion of the school district budget devoted to high-stakes testing, we would have money to hire the additional teachers.

It might not seem like CSR and high-stakes testing are related, but both take resources—people and money. States and school districts who are heavily invested in high-stakes testing should consider better uses for their resources.

ANONYMITY AND SCHOOL SIZE

The research on school size is more tentative than other research discussed in this book, because there are a large number of small, rural schools. These schools dilute the overall difference between good, small schools and larger schools. The research favoring small schools, however, is persuasive enough that we need to worry about the huge schools that exist in the country—for example, elementary schools with 2,000 students and high schools with more than 3,000 students.

When you pay particular attention to qualitative research on small schools, you begin to see that a major advantage of small schools is that it is difficult for a student to be anonymous. Kids cannot get lost, ignored, or passed over in a small school. Imagine how easy it is for a student to become anonymous in a high school with 3,000 students. This simple but powerful fact resonates loud and clear when one asks teachers and students in small schools how they feel about their school. Most educators seem to agree that small size is a necessary but insufficient factor in good schools.

HIGH-STAKES TESTS

If you are on a diet, stepping on the bathroom scale will not cause you to lose weight. Any sensible person would know this. Likewise, any sensible person would know that testing kids, and attaching high stakes to the results, will not cause students to learn more or cause teachers to teach better. This absurd belief is widespread, and it baffles me. In addition, the unintended consequences of high-stakes tests, namely, grade retention and increased dropout rates, simply compounds the idiocy.

COMPUTER ADAPTIVE TESTS

One bright spot in the area of assessment is computer adaptive testing (CAT). The Northwest Evaluation Association (http://nwea.org) is a consortium of states and school districts that has developed a method to use computers to quickly and accurately assess a student's achievement level in both reading and mathematics. The testing software uses a database of over 13,000 items that are validated by grade level and month. The software chooses questions for the student to answer. The software then adjusts the question difficulty up or down based on how many items the student misses or answers correctly. The process takes less than 30 minutes, and it is handled entirely by the software.

Both individual and classroom results are printed instantly. Because this is a quick, efficient process, testing a student several times a year is feasible and can be done to ensure that the student is making sufficient progress.

By using advanced assessment procedures like these, we can put testing back into its rightful role of helping teachers rather than of trying to control them.

WHAT ARE SCHOOLS FOR?

Nearly all of the research discussed in this book uses outcome measures that are related to academic achievement. It is easy to forget that schools may have a larger mission than preparing students to receive a college-prep diploma. It is always useful to return to the basic question of, what are schools for? Maybe our schools need to prepare more craftsmen, tradesmen, and service-sector workers. Maybe our schools should prepare people for wise child rearing.

A PARTING THOUGHT

It is fine to cherish your beliefs about education as long as you keep an open mind and as long as you are willing to change your beliefs.

About the Author

Royal Van Horn is a professor of education at the University of North Florida and a monthly columnist for *Phi Delta Kappan*—the most prestigious educational journal. *Kappan* has a circulation of about 110,000 and an acceptance rate of less than 5%. Over his fourteen years as a columnist, the author has proven his ability to communicate complicated ideas to lay readers. In his nearly 40 year career as an educator, the author has written over 150 articles and books.